GENDER AND PEACE IN TEXTBOOKS AND SCHOOLING PROCESSES

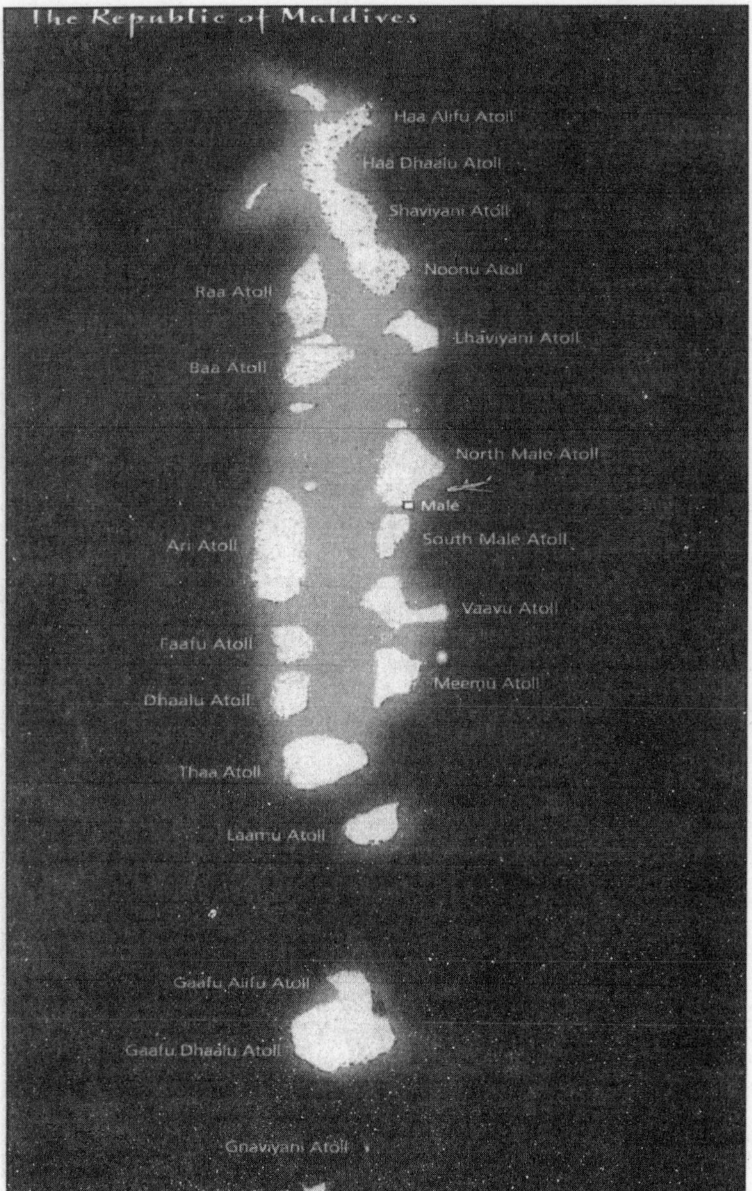

About the Book

The book *Gender and Peace in Textbooks and Schooling Processes : The Maldivian Experience,* is based on the project awarded by the Asian Scholarship Foundation (ASF) in 2006-2007 to undertake an in-depth study of textual and contextual situations in the Republic of Maldives. The study is based on exhaustive fieldwork conducted in Male and in the four Atolls—Noonu, Baa, Lhaviyani and Gaafu Alifu. The findings of the study highlights that in the scheme of promoting national identity, gender and peace are woven into textbooks of English, Environmental Studies and Social Studies, and in the schooling process itself. In connection with gender the policy, curriculum and syllabus address boys and girls. Textbooks of English, Environmental Studies and Social Studies, in their content depiction and visual portrayal, are gender inclusive, representing both sex and are gender neutral. Stereotyping is found in a limited way. Peace is projected more as a human value and Islamic religion as a repository of it. As a conflict management strategy, peace is dealt in a limited way in textual materials. In the context of classroom processes and co-curricular activities equal opportunities to participate are given to both sexes. Peace as a value is visibly portrayed in classrooms and in all important spaces outside classrooms. In connection with discipline issue there is no major problem in the Republic. The stress of handling minor discipline issue is on diagnostic, curative, corrective and reformatory aspects.

About the Author

Dr. Gouri Srivastava is Professor and Head, Department of Women's Studies, National Council of Education Research and Training (NCERT), New Delhi. Since completing her M.Phil at Jawaharlal Nehru University (JNU) and Ph.D. at Delhi University, she has published widely in academic journals at the National and International levels. Her books include *Women Who Created History : Exemplar Materials for Textbooks Writers and Teachers, Women's Higher Education in the 19th Century, Education in India : A Historical Perspective, The Legend Makers : Some Eminent Muslim Women of India, Women's Education in India : Issues and Dimensions, The Role of Begums of Bhopal in Promoting Education of Girls in the 19th and Mid 20th Century,* and *Women Role Models : Some Eminent Women of Contemporary India.* She is a recipient of scholarships from JNU, ICHR, ICSSR, George Eckert Institute for International Textbook Research, Braunschweig, Germany and from the Asian Scholarship Foundation at Bangkok.

Gender and Peace in Textbooks and Schooling Processes

The Maldivian Experience

Gouri Srivastava

CONCEPT PUBLISHING COMPANY PVT. LTD.
NEW DELHI-110 059

ISBN-13 : 978-81-8069-789-0

First Published 2012

Published and Printed by

Concept
Since 1974

Concept Publishing Company Pvt. Ltd.
Regd. Office :
A/15-16, Commercial Block, Mohan Garden
New Delhi-110059 (India)
Phones : 25351460, 25351794, *Fax :* 091-11-25357109
Email : publishing@conceptpub.com
Website : www.conceptpub.com

Editorial Office :
H-13, Bali Nagar, New Delhi-110 015, India.

Cataloging in Publication Data--*Courtesy:* D.K. Agencies (P) Ltd. <docinfo@dkagencies.com>

Srivastava, Gouri.
Gender and peace in textbooks and schooling processes : the Maldivian experience / Gouri Srivastava.
p. cm.
Includes bibliographical references (p.) and index.
ISBN 9788180697890

1. Sex role—Maldives—Textbooks. 2. Sex role—Study and teaching—Maldives. 3. Women and peace—Maldives—Textbooks. 4. Educational equalization—Maldives. 5. Women—Education—Maldives. 6. Sex differences in education—Maldives. 7. Education and state—Maldives. I. Title.

DDC 379.26095495 23

Maldives of My Vision

The dawn on a serene blue sky
the depth of the navy blue ocean
the dancing lapping waves
kindled in me hope and aspiration
of unravelling the mystique of the atoll nation Maldives!

*The enchanting islands with teeming, swarming dhonis**
the frolicking, backoning children
the loving, affectionate people
instilled in me confidence and courage
to sail through my cherished dream
of studying gender and peace.

Like the scenic dusk, an experience so soul fulfilling,
my pen wound up my thoughts on
facts of transcribing reality.

An inward journey of personhood
encourages me to move further
in the quest of yet another experience
of exploring the rich tapestry of an Asian subcontinent.

—Gouri Srivastava

* *Dhoni*—Local Boat

Foreword

Maldives, a picturesque archipelago state in the Indian Ocean, consisting of nearly 1200 small islands of which only 200 are inhabited, has been largely ignored by scholars. Little research has been done on these islands. *The Mystique of Maldives: A Study of Gender and Peace*, based on a research project on Gender and Peace: Education Policy, Curriculum, English, Environment Studies and Social Studies Textbooks of the Republic of Maldives, is therefore a pioneering work. This project was awarded to Professor Gouri Srivastava, Department of Women's Studies, National Council of Research and Training (NCERT), New Delhi, by the Asian Scholarship Foundation at Bangkok, in 2007.

This book looks at the schooling processes in the Republic of Maldives and has examined in detail textual and contextual situations from the perspective of gender and peace. The work is of utmost importance, especially in the context of Millennium Development Goals, as some of its parameters focus on achieving Education for All with parameters of equity, equality and quality. The book is largely based on qualitative data collected from extensive fieldwork done in Male and in four Atolls, viz. Noonu, Baa, Lhaviyani and Gaafu Alifu.

The findings of the study are important as they highlight that Maldives has achieved universalisation of primary education and the shift is now on 10 years of universal basic education by 2010. It has succeeded in forming unified national system of education with a common national curriculum. In the context of gender and peace the study depicts that in the scheme of promoting national identity, the schooling processes including textbooks weave the issue of gender and peace adequately. Peace is dealt more as a value rather than as conflict management strategies. Gender stereotyping is found in a limited way. While these achievements are very laudable in the domain of eduçation, Maldives, like most of the South Asian countries, faces a paradox between issues of quality and quantitative expansion in education while mechanism for addressing quality issues such as those related to infrastructure, introduction of motivational schemes, teaching learning processes, availability of resources in content areas, provision of ICT facilities and upgrading professionalism of teachers is being developed. The findings of the research highlight that a lot more focused efforts are needed for achieving MD Goals by 2015.

I congratulate Professor Gouri Srivastava for undertaking this research in Maldives. I am sure the findings of the study will be useful to the policy-makers of Maldives and to other neighbouring SAARC countries who are striving to achieve Education for All.

Aparna Basu
Formerly Professor of History
University of Delhi &
President, All India Women's Conference

Acknowledgements

The present book *The Mystique of Maldives: A Study of Gender and Peace* is a culmination of a research project awarded by the Asian Scholarship Foundation in 2007. The study highlights that the domain of implicit and explicit knowledge embedded in textual material and in the schooling processes weave the twin human issues and do not treat it as an add on approach. In the context of gender, glimpses of stereotyping are reflected in textbooks and in the schooling processes. Priority of the schooling ethos is on strengthening Islamic values in the children.

In this quest of unravelling the educational scenario of Maldives, I would especially like to mention my supervisor Professor Aparna Basu, former Professor of History, University of Delhi and President, All India Women's Conference, who has been a tremendous source of motivation and encouragement for undertaking the present project. I would particularly like to express my heartfelt gratitude to Professor Lourdes G. Salvador, Executive Director, Asian Scholarship Foundation, Bangkok whose inspiring words for all Asia Fellow of Cohort eight at the orientation programme held at Bangkok in July 1-4, 2006 gave me the much needed confidence to carry out this project in an unexplored region by an Asian scholar.

I express my thanks to the former Director of NCERT, Professor Krishna Kumar, who supported me in this endeavour.

This project could not have been carried out successfully without the support of the Government of Maldives who had extended generous cooperation in its completion.

I owe a debt of gratitude to all faculty members of the host institution, i.e. Educational Development Centre, Male

Republic of Maldives. In this regard I would specially like to thank Dr. Sheema Saeed, Director General, Dr. Naashia Mohamed, Former Assistant Director General, Ms. Fathimath Nahid Shakir, Curriculum Developer, Mr. Ahmed Shakeeb, Former Assistant Director General, Mr. Ali Najeeb, Former Deputy Director, Mr. Ahmed Yasir, Mr. Gulfishan Shafeeu, Ms. Shirumeen Ahmed, Hidaya Zahir.

I would also like to thank Senior Officials of the Ministry of Education who assisted me in data collection in Male and in the Islands. In this regard I would express my gratitude to Ms. Sameera Ali, Deputy Principal, Central Zone Coordinator and Mr. Ahmed Shafeeu, Director, Policy Planning and Research Section.

Special thanks are due to Ms. Aishath Shehenaz Adam, Executive Director, Educational Supervision and Quality Improvement Section and Ms. Faheema Mohamed, for giving me an opportunity to conduct school visits in different Islands of Maldives.

Thanks are also due to all the Principals of Schools in Male and in the Atolls visited for allowing me to conduct classroom observations and focus group discussions with teachers and students to get information on textual and contextual situations in the context of equity, equality and quality education. Photographs used in this book were generously provided by all the schools that were visited and in a few permission was given to take photographs. Thanks are due to Principals, Senior Assistant Principal, Deputy Principal and Supervisors and Teachers of Ghiyasuddin School, Imaduddin School, Iskandhar School, Jamaluddin School, Kalaafaanu School, Thaajuddin School, Almadharasathul Arabiyathul Islamiyya, Muhyiddin School, Fareedhiyya School, Aminiya School, Majeedhiya School, Dharumavantha School, Madhrasathul Ameer Ahmed, Madhrasathul Ahmadhiya, Galholhu Madharusa, Maafannu Madharusa, Fohdhoo, Kudafaree Madhrasa, Hidhaayaa, Madhrasa Ifthithaan Naifaru, Baa Atoll Educational Centre, Thulhaadhoo School and School at Gaafu Alifu Atoll.

For understanding the social milieu of Maldives the interactions with Naseema Mohamed, Special Advisor,

National Centre for Linguistic and Historical Research, Male, Naila Firdous, MD, DGO, Founder Member of Society for Health Education, Male and Habeeba Hussain Habeeb, Executive Director, National Library, Male were very useful and rewarding as they provided me with rich insight for understanding the social context of the present educational scenario in Maldives.

My project could not have been successfully completed without the constant support and encouragement of my parents and my family members. My husband Professor Ved Prakash Srivastava and my son Gaurav Prakash were pillars of strength and emotional support in my trying hours. My colleagues at the Department of Women's Studies kept me cheerful with their encouraging mails.

Last but not the least, I would like to mention Meenakshi Tomer, DTP operator for meticulously typing this manuscript.

— Gouri Srivastava

Contents

1

Introduction

The present decade has set an agenda for all countries of the world to achieve humane and sustainable development. This guiding philosophy has been embedded in the Millennium Development Goals (MDG). The thrust of the MDGs is to eliminate all kinds of paradoxes in society, i.e. between equity, equality and quality related issues, particularly in the domain of education, health and employment. In other words it envisions that all signatory countries work towards eliminating all forms of inequality in the context of class, gender and location, and work towards a global partnership. The Republic of Maldives has also chartered its development initiative in all its core sectors keeping in mind the philosophy of MDGs.

Maldives, earlier known as *Dhivehi Raajje,* is a unique picturesque Indian Ocean archipelagic state, consisting of 1,200 small coral islands out of which 200 are inhabited. The total area including land and sea is about 90,000 sq. km. The Dhivehi Raajje was familiar to travellers, seafarers, missionaries, traders since the ancient times. It was peopled for well over 2000 years. Presently it is 100% Sunni Muslim country. Islam is the religion of the state and the backbone of the society. Fishing has been and continues to be the main economic activity of the people; however tourism is now gradually acquiring an important edge in the employment sector.

The glimpses of the Republic can be ascertained from the travel accounts of people who had visited this island in different capacities. Their written accounts are an important primary source for knowing the life and condition of people who had inhabited this Island nation. The Islands are referred in the accounts of classical Arab and Chinese sources. Books that trace its historical cultural evolution are those written by Francois Pyrard, a Frenchman who was detained in this Island for five and a half years. He landed in Maldives due to shipwreck. His accounts are important for knowing the Maldivian society, specially the status of women. In his book he mentions that girls in the Republic married at the age of 15 and boys could marry whenever they wanted. H.C.P. Bell's book on Maldives titled *The Maldive Islands : Monograph on the History, Archaeology and Epigraphy*, is a very important source documenting the polity, economy and the social milieu. This book encompasses accounts of his stay in Maldives in three different years, i.e. in 1879 due to shipwreck, in 1920 as a visitor and in 1922 on being deputed by the Government of Ceylon to study Maldivian Buddhist antiquities. His scholarly work was published posthumously and till date is regarded as an important literature in knowing the Maldivian society. Besides these pioneering works, more recently, a book by Naseema Mohamed on *Essays on Early Maldives* meticulously documents the early sources on ancient Maldives. This book has also highlighted a need for conducting extensive research, including scientific excavations of archaeological sites, for gaining a clearer picture about the country's pre-Islamic past.

Contemporary available printed materials that are relevant to the present study include the *Statistical Yearbook of Maldives: 2006*. This book gives a detailed account of gender disaggregated data on demography and education and is important in getting information, particularly on enrolments, divorce and the employment scenario in the Republic. In the context of gender there is a publication titled, *Achievements and Challenges in Maldives in connection with Convention on the Elimination of All Forms of Discrimination against Women*. This document gives an overview about the status of women in Maldives and the existing laws and rights that govern them. *The Seventh National Development Plan 2006-2010*, in its section on education, gives the current scenario of the country's education policy and related strategy to achieve the MDGs. *Strengthening the Framework of Education towards Vision 2020* envisions the kind of education the country wants to develop for its citizens. Textbooks published by the Educational Development Centre are an important publications for school children at the primary level and an important and crucial secondary source for the study.

The unpublished literature includes reports and papers brought out by the Ministry of Education and the Educational Development Centre. The Ministry had compiled a paper on Education Policy, Vision and Strategy. This paper gives the government policy on education. Materials brought out by the Educational Development Centre were extremely important in the context of the present project. They were the Draft Curriculum Framework (1999) and the syllabi of English (2004), Social Studies (1990) and Environment Studies (1990). Report on the Gender Analysis of Primary Textbooks (Shakir, Nahid, Fathimath, Yasir Ahmed, 2007) was especially relevant, as it mentions how gender is dealt in the textual materials. The analysis of this report highlighted that there is gender bias in primary books. However, the findings of the present study indicate that it is stereotyping that is found in textual materials. In a very limited way biases are reflected.

More recent publications on Maldives are mainly devoted to tourism. The phrases used in these materials are mainly promotional in nature and contain catchy slogans. Maldives is very often mentioned in these materials as the Pearl of Indian Ocean, a tourist paradise and an enchanting retreat. Phrases commonly used to describe this Island nation in the print and the audio visual media highlight the sunny side of Maldives. These materials make a very passing reference to education, economy and the society.

In fact books, research articles etc. on South Asia of late hardly make a mention of Maldives. World Maps have also ignored this strategically located Republic. Very few publications make a mention of it, e.g. UNICEF report on *Status of World Children* and some publications on SAARC countries. Recent reference to Maldives in the print media is in the context of global warming and its impact on the physical location of this Island Republic. Many scientists and environmentalists predict the gradual extinction of this pearl in the Indian Ocean due to climatic changes and rising sea level. In fact, the occurrence of Tsunami in 2004 has already resulted in the submergence of some of its Islands.

While the available literature about this Island Republic is scant, those that depict it are important and relevant in connection with the present study. They do help in unravelling the socio-economic and education systems existing in the past and the present. In the context of gender and peace, they are crucial as they highlight the positioning of men and women in the Maldivian society in the context of roles and responsibilities and how power relationships are gradually shaped and constructed in the family and in the society. In the context of peace, they help in knowing how Maldivian society prioritises peace. It is more in the context of value rather than as a strategy for addressing social and political conflicts.

Published and unpublished works on Maldives together weave the rich tapestry of *Dhivehi Raajje* and provide an important backdrop to the research.

The present book is a pioneering work of in depth understanding of how gender and peace are reflected in textual materials and in the schooling processes in the Republic of Maldives. The finding of the study highlights that schooling processes prioritise promoting national identity among children. The twin parameters, i.e. gender and peace are woven into textual materials and contextual situations.

In the context of gender, under education policy, curriculum and syllabus address both sexes. Textual materials pertaining to the domains of English, Environment Studies and Social Studies in their content depiction and visual portrayal are mainly gender inclusive and neutral. Stereotyping as mentioned earlier is found in a limited way. Classroom processes strengthen inclusive activities for both genders. Classroom management, pedagogical processes and in all curriculum plus activities, equal opportunities are provided to both genders. Children with behaviour problems are not stigmatised by the school management or by the supervisors and teachers. Corporal punishment is banned in the Republic.

In the context of peace, textual materials stress on peace as a human value and Islamic religion as its repository. As a strategy for addressing social tensions and conflicting situations in the family and society, the focus of all textual material is very limited. In the context of classroom process, a similarity in approach was found. Peace is dealt more as human values that needed to be instilled in students from primary years. In school and classroom observations and quotations on peace by eminent persons were put at the entrance of the school, in the classrooms, on the bulletin boards and in the corridors. The code of conduct expected from students and teachers for strengthening harmonious relations between sexes was mentioned in the Students Handbooks that were available in all schools. For creating a congenial environment in schools the handbooks also stress upon behaviour patterns, once again expected from teachers and students, along with dress code and hair style for boys and girls.

In connection with conflict management and social tensions, effort of all schooling processes which included government and private, stressed on diagnostic, curative and reformatory aspects. Disciplinary issues were collectively dealt by all stakeholders.

The methodology adopted in the present study was mainly qualitative in nature. It was limited to the analysis of textual materials of English, Environmental Studies and Social Studies. An evaluation tool (given in the appendix) was used to examine the books from the perspective of Gender and Peace. For examining the relationship between textual materials and contextual situations, fieldwork was carried out in 24 co-educational and single sex schools in Male and four atolls, i.e. Noonu, Baa, Lhaviyani and *Gaafu Alifu*. In these schools classroom processes and co-curricular activities have been examined with the help of an observation tool. The total number of classroom observations conducted was 87 in primary and lower secondary grades. Generally three observations per school were done. In Muhyiddin School four classes were observed and in Madhrasathul Ifthithaah and in Baa Atoll Educational Centre 12 classes were observed. In the last Atoll, classes could not be observed as the school was closed. Classroom observations were limited to content areas related to the domain of English, Social Studies and Environmental Studies. In secondary classes History, Geography, Economics, Commerce and English were observed. Co-curricular activities were observed in four primary schools in Male and two schools in Baa and Lhaviyani Atolls. Interview schedules were canvassed to 24 school Principals/Assistant Principals. Schedules were also canvassed to 96 male and female teachers. Four male and female teachers per school were selected randomly. Group discussions were held with six to eight teachers and similar number of students in each school, to elicit their perceptions on gender and peace. In addition, discussions were also held with some eminent persons like Naseema Mohamed, Special Advisor, National Centre for Linguistic and Historical Research and Dr. Naila Firdous founder member of the Society for Health and Education. Some of the limitations of the study relate to non-availability of published materials and gender disaggregated data on repeaters in different grades. Another limitation was that all Atolls and schools in the Island could not be visited.

The present book consists of four chapters. The first chapter is the introduction to the study, the second chapter mentions in detail the analysis of government developed textual materials used at the primary stages, from the perspective of gender and peace.

The third chapter is set in school and classroom settings in Male and in a few Islands that were visited. In depth observations of pedagogical processes, including children's participation in curriculum and curriculum plus activity, are discussed.

The fourth chapter gives a vivid portrayal of status of women in the past and in the present times in Maldives.

The last chapter gives a graphic account of challenges that the Republic of Maldives faces, especially in the domain of education. This relates to the phenomena regarding quality issues in education that need to be addressed substantially for achieving the Millennium Development Goals.

2

Gender and Peace

A Study of Textual Materials in the Republic of Maldives

Textbooks are the most popular teaching aid used in the teaching and learning process. They are storehouses of implicit knowledge centred on time, space and institution. Textbooks are also repository of values, beliefs and norms upheld by different nations of the world. Textbooks and teachers are together kernel of secondary agent of socialisation that has a substantial influence on the overall personality development of children.

The present century is on the threshold of globalisation, liberalisation and it is marked by an explosion in the arena of information technology. This phenomenon has impacted all cultures and societies of the developed and developing worlds. These contemporary changes have led to dismantling of temporal and spatial boundaries and have facilitated the movement of people, ideas and commodities all over the world. In the realm of education these changes have impacted the domain of implicit knowledge embedded in textual materials. The strait-jacketed boundaries between science and social science have gradually narrowed down giving way to applied disciplines with greater stress on the use of information technology. While these changes have been visibly felt in the overall domain of education, it is important to see how knowledge pertaining to different disciplines at the school stage responds to this techno savvy revolution. In the context of

South Asia, textbooks and other supplementary materials are popular teaching aids and are largely accessible to all children.

Textual materials are designed to tell children what their elders want them to know. Textbooks are repositories of historical images and events that are centred on time, space and institutions. The manner in which events are woven vary from country to country. It is assumed and often documented that school textbooks tend to reflect the dominant ideas, beliefs, opinions, attitudes, values and norms in the society or the community. In other words they depict the ideas and values of hegemonic groups and their by become vehicles of disseminating cultural capital. For details refer Giroux (1981). Several studies in the domain of textbook analysis such as Yuette (2000), Kumar (2001) and Srivastava (2005) have highlighted that in the scheme of promoting national identities, very often there is a tendency on the part of textbook authors to depict neighbouring country or countries having shared common past in a limited and prejudicial manner. Perhaps this is mainly done to justify the country's own national viewpoint. Also, to instil national consciousness and patriotic feeling among children, chronology of events are not correctly portrayed by textbook writers', particularly in subjects like social sciences.

Among the subjects that constitute social sciences such as History, Geography, Economics and Sociology, the subject that is impacted mostly by subjective interpretation is History. This is especially true when one examines the history section of textbooks of Social Studies of Pakistan, wherein one finds that authors tend to selectively choose historical events to justify the creation of an independent state. Textbooks have always been instrumental in legitimising countries, standpoint and ideologies. The content and form of school textbooks as cultural objects are determined by social factors, such as the socio-political order, the level of modernisation and the value system. School textbooks are ordained to transmit values and ideologies to the next generation, that is, to be socially constitutive. The manner in which knowledge is constructed in the domain of each subject area impacts the attitude and values of children. It also leaves enduring images in them regarding their country and the world at large. In the context of gender and peace the manner in which textual materials depict the role of men and women either strengthen stereotypes and biases, or promote values of gender justice, harmony and peace.

The centrality of gender and peace in educational discourses have acquired pivotal place in the education policy of each country since the 1990s. Both the parameters have highlighted the increasing concern of the academia on growing gender disparities in education and the increasing phenomena of physical and emotional violence that nearly all societies of developed and developing world are currently facing. In 1997 Mahbub-ul-Haq stated that the South Asian Region was the most gender insensitive in the world. According to him, it is the only region with a sex ratio of less than 100 women for every hundred men; a region with 22% of the world population, but 45% of the world maternal mortality, highest rate of female illiteracy and greatest proportion of girls out of school Hayword, R.F. (2000) stated that other than violence the region is affected by growing trafficking in women, drug peddling, cross border terrorism and ethnic violence that has eroded the human face of development in this region. This phenomenon has also impacted the delicate balance between human activity and nature, resulting in degradation of the environment. In fact, these turbulent human activities have made educationalists apprehensive about achieving sustainable human development in the region. Therefore, there is a growing concern among the educationalists, policy planners and administrators on evolving strategies that would help in addressing problems that the South Asian region faces in contemporary times.

In the domain of education, peace and gender issues have acquired critical concern, both in text and contextual situations. Regarding peace, there is a gradual shift from seeing peace in a restrictive manner, i.e. seeing it only as a human value or as a means for addressing internal and external wars. It is now gradually seen as an effective strategy for addressing conflicts and social tensions plaguing the delicate fabric of the society. The focus is now on peace building processes in the school curriculum, textbooks and classroom processes. Regarding gender, the thrust is now on weaving gender as a human issue in all disciplines, so that values of caring and sharing, dignity of labour, learning to live together, valuing women's contributions and many more are translated in all disciplines in the content, visuals and exercises. The approach is to see peace and gender as integral parts of textual materials and not as an add on approach. The focus of the author is to see whether these concerns are embedded in all disciplines so that it is effectively transmitted to children.

In the present chapter an effort is made to see how both the parameters are addressed in textual materials developed in the Republic of Maldives.

The early feminist researches of the 1960s found that the voices of girls/women were missing in the plethora of textual materials that were generated the world over. They were of the view that women's oppression since 1960 could be understood as their silencing, and hence their marginalisation in historical and other related literatures. Therefore, the focus was on finding women's voices in different disciplines. Researches since 1960s and 1970s in the context of women adopted the 'add women and stir' approach. In fact inclusion was done at a very superficial level in the textual materials. This led to the adoption of biographical approaches in including the contributions of women in a very brief manner in different disciplines without highlighting their trials and struggles. Textual materials failed to see women's contributions in the context specific situations or weave their work into content, visuals and illustrations. This method of discussing women's contributions in very superficial manner continued till the 1990s and is largely found in textual materials of South Asian region which include Pakistan, Bangladesh and Nepal.

Textbooks produced by the government agencies, especially in SAARC region, were coloured by this approach. In this context studies on textual materials pertaining to South Asia such as Pakistan, Bangladesh and Nepal have highlighted the low priority that has been given to gender and peace. As stated earlier the approach adopted in the context of gender was 'add women and stir'. Texts ignored to portray the contributions of women in different fields such as agriculture and all service sectors of the economy. Stress was mainly given to facts and events that strengthen national identity. The discussion on time, space and institution focused more on hegemonic institutions and ideas that negate the voices of the common people including women. In this regard Srivastava (2005, 2006) in her papers has emphasised the marginalisation of women's contributions in the content and visuals in Social Studies textbooks developed by the government agencies of some of the South Asian countries, viz. Pakistan, Bangladesh and Nepal. Analysis of textbooks from the perspective of peace as a strategy of conflict management and social tension was very limited and perhaps considered not very important. In this context Ruth (2000) mentions the important role of education in addressing the growing violence against women in South Asia. One of the strategies suggested by her was promoting gender inclusive curriculum and its transaction. There is also a mention of the role of schooling processes in inculcating among students skills of negotiation and consensus in addressing conflicting situations in schools. A publication by Tawil, Sobhi and Alexandra (2004) situates education in societies affected by internal turmoil such as, Northern Ireland, Lebanon, Mozambique, Sri Lanka, Rwanda and Bosnia, to see how education can contribute in reconstructing and renewing social peace based on justice. In this regard effort is made by the author to examine the role of education policy, and of curriculum in particular, in their capacity to erode or reinforce social cohesion.

The present chapter is a step in this direction. Attempt is to examine how the textual materials produced by the government agencies weave internal concerns of gender and peace in the textbooks of English, Environmental Studies and Social Studies in the Republic of Maldives. The analysis of textual material also attempts to examine whether the textual material follows an add on approach or integrate the twin parameters.

In the realm of education Maldives has succeeded in forming a unified national system of education with a common national curriculum. An initial examination of the government policy depicts that gender and peace are woven into it. This is portrayed in some of the statements of the education policy that is also the guiding philosophy for preparation of textual materials. Excerpts of the policy—

"Providing school education to Maldivians, both formally as well as informally, currently the emphasis of the government policy is geared towards expanding and improving the quality of basic education through consideration of the relevance and outcome of structure, content and process of basic education, expanding secondary education opportunities in an equitable manner across the country, introducing vocational technical education at school level, developing higher secondary education and diversifying educational opportunities for youth and adults through non-formal education."

Further, in the context of gender, the Seventh National Development Plan 2006-2010, Vol. 1, Policies and Strategies once again reiterates gender concerns. It depicts that—

"Ensure that all children irrespective of gender, ability and location have access to quality basic education ...." (p. 115)

Regarding peace, the above-mentioned document states the organisation of national campaigns to raise students' awareness on nutrition, reproductive health and life skills. For operationalising this parameter of the policy some of the listed strategies are very relevant in the case of conflict management and social tensions. They are—

- Implement Child Rights and anti-bullying policies in all schools.
- Develop school-community capacity in promoting safe behaviour for reproductive health.
- Develop school-community capacity in promoting physical development and fitness among children.
- Develop school-community capacity in life skills. (p. 116)

The Ministry of Education Strategic Plan 2004-2005, in its section on "Make the school the most appropriate environment for teaching and learning" also has in-built mention of peace in some of its listed strategies. They are—

1.2 Distribute facilities to all schools equally
1.3 Provide equal access to education for all students
1.4 Make the Maldivian school a role model of discipline-friendly, united and cooperative society
1.5 Make the learning environment be happy, safe, loving and caring
1.6 Make the school a place where healthy living is encouraged.

(Ministry of Education Strategic Plan 2004-05)

Gender and Peace are also reflected in the vision and mission statement of education. On education the vision states the following—

> *"Every Maldivian will have access to quality primary and secondary education and training. The education provided will promote maximum realisation of individual potential while at the same time instilling religious and cultural values that will foster social unity and harmony, and love and pride in the nation. Maldivians will be endowed with necessary knowledge and skills to be productive, able and active participants both in the national and international arena."*
>
> (Ministry of Education, Republic of Maldives)

For implementing the policy parameter and vision into practice, a draft framework of the National Curriculum came into practice in 1999. The purpose of the framework is to help design and implement all activities in school in the primary and secondary levels. The framework of the national curriculum is based on the national philosophy that is gender inclusive. It states—

> *Any student who completes the Maldivian education is entitled to get the ability to assist and promote his/her Island and country. In order to safeguard the Islamic belief system and the Maldivian nationality, a child's social, emotional, moral and economic maturity should be developed and skills to do this should be taught. He/She is entitled to this as a member of the Islamic Maldivian Community and as an Individual.*
>
> (Ministry of Education, Republic of Maldives)

The objectives of the draft national curriculum have also strands of gender and peace. It seeks to address both sexes for promoting their physical, mental and expressive aspects. For weaving the philosophy of curriculum in different disciplinary areas, syllabuses have been designed and prepared. In the context of English and Maths the syllabuses have been revised to outcome-based ones during the years 2004 and 2005. The syllabuses of the other subjects are under preparation. In the present study the syllabuses of some subjects that have been consulted are—English syllabus draft-2004, Environmental Studies-1990 and Social Studies-1990.

In connection with English, the syllabus is gender inclusive. Terms like students is constantly used. Since the syllabus is outcome-based, it stresses on what the students know and what they can do as a result of instruction. The main focus of the syllabus is on helping students to develop their reading, writing, speaking and listening skills. There is a mention in the syllabus of how language can develop the student's ability to participate in a wide range of classroom activities including discussions, debates, group, pair work and project work.

In the context of peace, the objectives of the syllabus focus on developing the self, i.e. confidence, independence and enjoyment as effective users of English. One can deduce from the objective that the syllabus strengthens the value of learning to learn together, sharing and caring, and peer group interactions.

The Environmental studies syllabus stresses on the development of awareness, knowledge, attitude and skills among students about their immediate and global environment. The focus is on promoting harmonious link between human activity and nature by adopting a problem solving strategy. It attempts to inculcate in students the necessary skills for sustainable development. These skills relate to critical thinking, decision-making, communication, analytical observation, negotiation and conflict resolution which the students can apply in their daily life situations.

In connection with peace, the syllabus focuses on promoting environment sensitivity among boys and girls, inculcating in them values of preservation and conservation of nature and leading a healthy life.

The Social Studies syllabus also has components of gender and peace. Inclusive terms like human activities and humans are constantly used. Once again the significant area that is emphasised is focusing on human activities *vis-a-vis* nature. Besides this the evolution of humans, working of contemporary social institutions etc. are stated. In the context of conflict management it is greenhouse effect that is given more space. For the purposes of analysis of textual materials, an evaluation tool had been prepared from the perspective of gender and peace. Only those textbooks developed by government agencies, i.e. Educational Development Centre, Male of grades 1–7 have been examined.

Analysis of Textbooks

Textbooks belonging to different disciplinary areas are an important teaching aid in the Republic. The content, visuals, suggested activities and questions in the textual materials mirror the values and beliefs upheld by the society. The domain of implicit knowledge embedded in the textbooks pertaining to different disciplinary areas reflects the philosophy of the nation. The textbooks analysed in the present chapter are those related to the disciplines of English, Environment Studies and Social Studies. Books at the primary level are prepared by government agency, i.e. Education Development Centre (EDC). At a preliminary glance of the textbooks it appears that priority is given to strengthening national identity and Islamic values in children. This is clearly depicted on the cover pages of all textbooks, particularly in selection of visuals and the use of *Dhivehi* script. In the context of the content of all textbooks, the selections of themes also strengthen national identity. Symbolic use of visuals and content representing the natural habitat of Maldives, *Dhivehi* script, tangible part of its cultural heritage, people and there lifestyle depict that contextualisation has been taken into account by all the authors.

English Textbooks

In the Republic of Maldives English is the medium of instruction. It is also taught as an independent subject. At the primary level the English textbooks focus on promoting speaking, listening, reading and writing skills among children. At the later stages the stress is more on reading, writing, speaking, listening and the development of vocabulary. The textbooks analysed in the present paper are those prescribed for grades 1-7. The English textbooks at this level mainly consist of series of English Core Readers and The New English Pupils Books for each grade. The Pupil's Book for each grade is a workbook for students wherein different forms of literary exposition such as passage writing, essay, using pictures to answer questions, drawing, penning down thoughts in the form of poems and prose, writing correct grammatical sentences etc. are emphasised.

In Grade 1, there are no Core Readers, instead a set of 34 books are prescribed. They are English for Us: Easy to Read series. These books are mainly pictographic in nature having very little content. In grades 2 to 5 there are a set of 19 Core Readers. In each grade there are a set of 5 books except Grade 5 that has 2 books and grades 6 and 7 that have 1 each. All grades have one Pupil's Book except Grade 1 that has two

Fig. 2.1 : Gender inclusive visuals

Source: Cover page of English for Us, Education Development Centre, Male, 2005

Pupils' Books. In Grade 2 there is an addition of a supplementary workbook. The Core Readers and Pupils Books have been printed from 2003-2007. The first edition of Easy to Read Series was published in 2005. All the textbooks are authored by women except Grade 1 textbooks where two men are also authors.

An analysis of textbooks grade-wise from the point of gender representation in visuals depicts that in Grade 1, the English for Us: Easy to Read series has 49.4% visuals that are gender inclusive, 38.4% represent either boys or girls. These visuals are not biased as they are in tune with the context specific situations. 12.2% are gender neutral representing the natural habitat of Maldives. In Pupils Books of this grade the visuals are mainly gender neutral, i.e. 56.8. Those representing either boys or girls are 27.7%. Only 15.6% are gender inclusive.

Gender Analysis

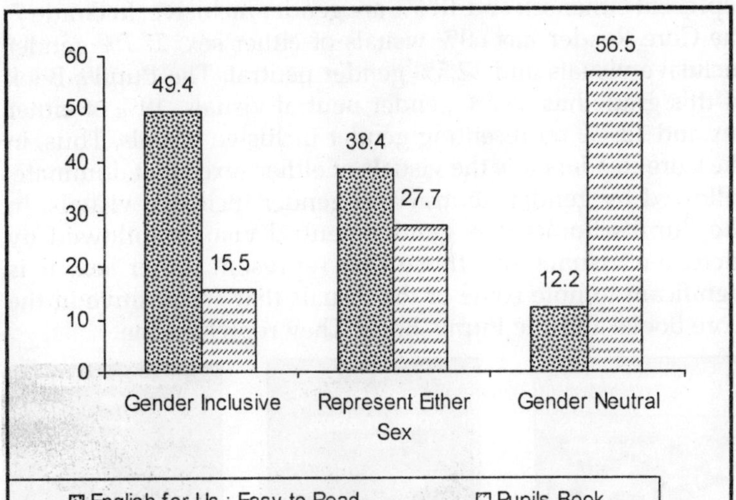

In Grade 2, English Core Readers have 48.3% visuals portraying either boys or girls, 37.7% are gender neutral and 14.4% gender inclusive. The pupil's books have 57.7% visuals that are gender neutral, 30.9% are gender inclusive and 11.4% represent either of the sexes. The supplementary book has 56.8% gender neutral visuals, 27.6% represent either boys or girls and 15.6% are gender inclusive visuals. In Grade 3, the English Core Readers have 63.4% visuals that represent either sex, 20.5% are gender inclusive and 16.1% are gender neutral. The Pupil's Book of this grade has 85.8% visuals that are gender neutral, 9.4% are gender inclusive and 4.7% represent either sex. In Grade 4, the English Core Readers have 44.2% visuals that represent either sex, 38.4% are gender inclusive and 17.4% are gender neutral. The Pupil's Books of this grade have 79.5% visuals that are gender neutral, 12.1% are gender inclusive and 8.4% represent either boys or girls. In Grade 5, 55.7% visuals are gender neutral, 29.5% represent either sex and 14.8% visuals are gender inclusive. The Pupil's Books of these grade have 55.85% visuals that are gender neutral, 25.6% represent either sex and 18.6% are gender inclusive. In Grade 6, the visuals in The English Core Reader represent 40% visuals of either sex, 35.6% are gender neutral and 24.4% are gender inclusive. In Pupil's Book, 47.7% visuals are gender neutral, 33.7% visuals represent either sex and 18.6% are gender inclusive. In Grade 7, the Core Reader has 60% visuals of either sex, 27.7% gender inclusive visuals and 12.5% gender neutral. The Pupil's Book of this grade has 68.6% gender neutral visuals, 19% of either sex and 12.4% representing gender inclusive visuals. Thus, in the Core Readers it is the visuals of either sexes that dominate, followed by gender neutral and gender inclusive visuals. In the Pupil's Books it is gender neutral visuals followed by inclusive visuals and those that represent either sex. It is significant to note some of the visuals that are positive in the Core books and the Pupils Book. They represent the

Fig. 2.2

Source : Cover pages of English Core Reader Grade I, II and III (2004-2006), Male.

Gender Analysis

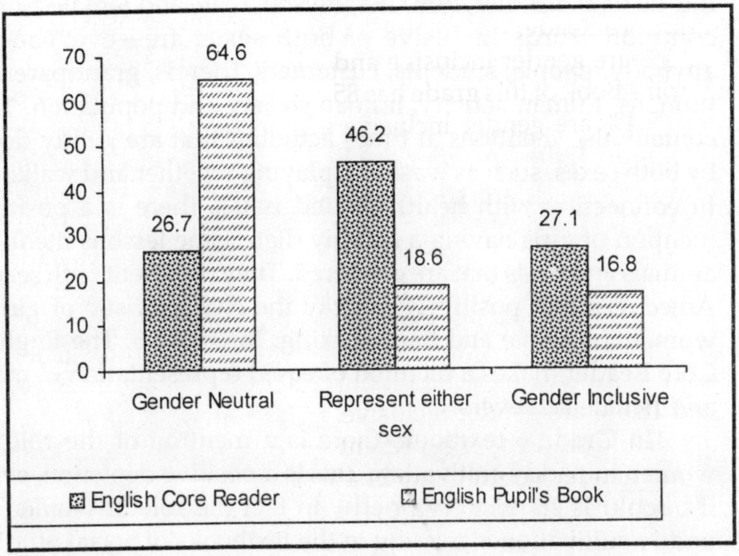

following—*household chores being performed by both sexes, cleaning the classroom, a joint venture of boys and girls, experimenting, studying, playing, enjoying leisure, driving a vehicle, climbing a mountain and rowing a boat.*

Visuals depicting men and women in familial roles are those linked with *masculine* and *feminine* traits. Women are shown in household chores such as washing, cooking, cleaning, taking care of the siblings and nursing. The professions that women are associated with are an extension of their domestic sphere such as teaching, nursing, florist and typist. Visuals depict men as fishers, farmers, bankers, carpenters, police personnel, doctors, sportsmen, chemists, mechanics, athletes, tobacconists, greengrocers, postmen and news agents. All outdoor games are associated with boys, such as football, swimming, flying kites and cycling. Girls on the other hand are shown in all indoor activities such as praying, playing with dolls, singing and dancing. Some of the manual skills are also associated with men. They are making hammers, using ladder, glue, bricks, screwdriver, plug point and holding a saw.

The content of all the English textbooks use terms that represent both sexes. They are—you, your, they, them, us, we, me, he/she, his/her, him/her, myself, male and female. Some common words inclusive of both sexes are—everybody, anybody, people, students, customers, friends, grandparents, humans, human activity, human society and population. The content also mentions at times activities that are jointly done by both sexes, such as washing, playing together and walking. In connection with health related issues there is a positive mention of girls having a healthy diet. Some lessons mention animals and birds that are gendered. They represent both sexes. Adjectives that positively portray the characteristic of girls/women are brave and hardworking. In Grade 5, The English Core Reader makes a mention of equal representation of male and female achievers.

In Grade 6 textbook, there is a mention of the role of women in paddy cultivation. This is a positive depiction, even though it is stated very briefly. In fact the role of women in paddy cultivation is missing in the textbooks of Social Studies of neighbouring countries such as Pakistan, Nepal and Bangladesh. In Pupil's Book of the same grade, there is a paragraph reflecting the positive status of the women in Maldives. It mentions that men and women enjoy equal property rights in the Republic. There is also a reference to women as head of government in Maldives' known history. Positive strands are also found in Grade 7 Core Reader. There is a mention of the changing status of women from homemakers to professionals. In one context in the same book, there is a mention of Islamic religion stressing on the acquisition of knowledge by both sexes. In addition, the credit of the revival of the traditional Maldivian craft is mentioned as the joint contribution of both sexes. Besides, these positive references, some examples of women empowerment are stated, e.g. women questioning her ascribed status and being treated as second class citizen. Some of the stereotypical references found in connection with the content relate to the adjectives that are used for women. They are—beautiful, chaste, lovely, tall and slim, silly, reasonable, worried, efficient, elegant, merry, and adorable. For men it is—smart, active, energetic, enthusiastic and daring. Sometimes, the choice of the story also has elements of stereotyping, e.g. the legend of the daring Robin Hood, Mel sine—a fairy princess in the French legend, Cindrella and the Little Mermaid. Interestingly activities and project work designed in the textbooks are meant for both the sexes.

In the context of Peace the focus of the textbooks is more on promoting peace as a human value. Values such as sharing and caring, learning to live healthy, addressing everyone respectfully, equality between sexes, being honest and truthful and valuing women's contribution are focused upon. There is also mention of a few proverbs in the textual materials. In connection with conflicts and social tensions, family as an important social site is mentioned. For resolving conflicts in the family messages embedded in Islamic religion are stated to be the only solution. This is because religion is the harbinger of peace, forgiveness, success and happiness.

The textbooks of Environmental Studies of Grades 1 to 5 have an author team comprising six females and four males. The books have been published during 1998-2007. The different thematic areas of all the five books follow a pattern that focuses on the people, the earth, living things, the changing world and interdependence. For purposes of analysis of visuals and content of the five textbooks dealing with similar thematic area, the approach followed was initially to examine them individually and then collectively. From an in depth analysis of the textbooks of Environmental Studies it is seen that 67.23%

Gender Analysis

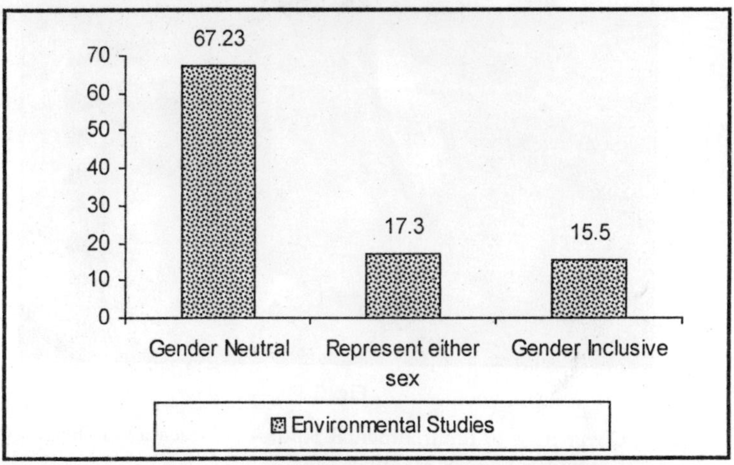

visuals are gender neutral, followed by 17.23% of visuals that represent either sex and 15.54% that are gender inclusive.

Some of the visuals in the textbooks are positive. They represent boys and girls eating a healthy diet, vacations being enjoyed by both sexes, experiments being conducted by boys and girls jointly. Playing, studying, handling modern means of communication and exercising are activities that are shown as gender inclusive.

Fig. 2.3

Source : Cover page of Environmental Studies 1, Educational Development Centre Republic of Maldives, 2006.

Visuals that are stereotypical show women in familial professions such as teaching and nursing and in roles that are part of the household chores. In connection with the content of the textbooks, the language used makes reference to terms that represent both the genders. They are—myself, my, our, you, yours, they, them and us. Common words representing both genders such as child, children, people, family, grandparents, Maldivian, tourist, human brain, human body, humans, students, everybody, friends, class representative, adult, elderly people and scientists are commonly used. Proper names of characters representing both the sexes are mentioned but they are done in context specific situations. Terms that represent relationships in the context of men are—he, his, father and uncle. For women it is—mother, she, her and sister. At times even the animal species are gendered. There is a reference to male fish and rat and the lion king who is a male. In the context of females it is the female rat, turtle and mosquitoes.

In the context of occupations the content makes a mention of some tailor-made professions for men and women which are similar to the English textbooks. Men are associated with outdoor occupations such as tourism and fishing, and women with nursing and mat making. Further, adjectives used for women are a bit stereotypical, e.g. wonderful cook. The activities and project work mentioned in the textbooks are meant for both the sexes.

In the context of peace the stress of the textbooks is on depicting peace as a value. Some human values such as sharing and caring, cherishing diversities, maintaining health and hygiene, leading a routine life and messages like *smoking is injurious to health* are referred. Conservation and preservation of habitat is stated in a limited manner. In connection with conflict management, the Environmental Studies textbooks mention some crucial steps that need to be taken for preventing the greenhouse effect and the phenomena of global warming. In the context of Maldives there is a brief mention of some strategies to protect the fragile environment. There is a mention of the successful million tree programme, awareness generation programmes on using alternate fuels other than firewood, discouraging the use of plastic bags, protecting the coral reef and keeping the Islands clean. However, the role of people, particularly women, in conserving and preserving the natural habitat of Maldives is not focused upon. Peace is also seen as a successful strategy in helping Maldives to have good relations with Asian countries. In the context of managing certain social tensions arising out of vehicular accidents in Male, there is a brief reference to laws enacted for its prevention.

The textbooks of Social Studies of grades 6 and 7 have subjects encompassing the disciplines of Geography, History, Political Science, Economics and Sociology. In the organisation of different thematic areas the textbooks of these grades follow an interesting pattern. In Grade 6, the pattern followed is—space (geography), time (history) and institutions (socio-economic and political). In Grade 7, the pattern is—time and then institutions. Both the textbooks have been re-printed in 2007. The author team of Grade 6 textbook comprises two females and for grade 7 it is an equal representation of both the genders, i.e. three males and three females. For purposes of analysis, visuals and content in each grade have been analysed separately and then collectively represented. Both the grades textbooks stress on visuals that are gender neutral; 69.4% visuals represent maps, diagrams, solar system, the animal kingdom, photographs of places and buildings, historical monuments and sites, inscriptions and coinage, the flora and the fauna and manufacturing industries etc.; 21.10% visuals represent either male or female. They are context specific as they mention personalities and people associated with different events and historical movements in relation to the world and Maldives in particular. Gender inclusive visuals are very limited. Only 9.04% visuals depict both sexes.

Visuals that are positive mention women in legislature (people's *majlis*), beaching a *dhoni* (traditional boat) and as heads of state. Some of the performing activities such as experiments are associated with both the sexes.

The content of the Social Studies textbooks of both grades makes use of terms that are gender inclusive. They are—you, your, themselves, they, we, us, our, their, he/she, him/her,

Fig. 2.4

Source : Social Studies 2, Third Edition, Grade 7, Education Development Centre, Male.

Gender Analysis

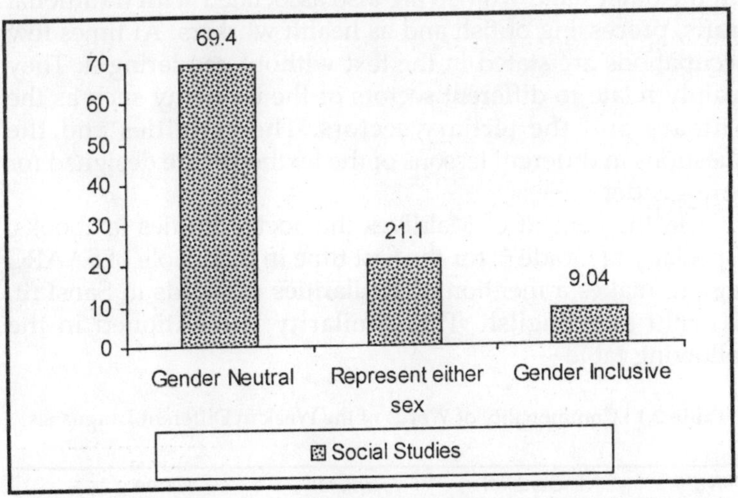

and persons. Some common words representing both sexes are—Maldivian, people, humans, human beings, human laws, humanity, human sufferings, human activity, human population, human space, human life, human brain, human muscle, male and female relationship, population, grandparents, working class, farming communities and scientists. The content of both the textbooks also makes a mention of names of personalities related to both the sexes. In connection with men, terms depicting relationships are used such as he, his, himself and mankind. For women it is her, she, girl, daughter and mother. The names of women rulers of Maldives are also stated. The adjectives used for men are famous, successful, fine and wise ruler. For women it is extremely limited. *Qualities* associated with women is charitable.

The roles in which men are projected are—rulers, historical and contemporary leaders, producers, social reformers and prophets. Interestingly, in the context of women there is a mention of them as leaders of countries both historically and in contemporary times. It is significant to note that leadership qualities are associated with both sexes. In connection with occupation, the content makes reference to men associated with fishing and being part of the traditional crafts of Maldives and as producers of different commodities. On the other hand women are also associated with traditional crafts, processing of fish and as health workers. At times few occupations are stated in the text without gendering it. They mainly relate to different sectors of the economy such as the primary and the tertiary sectors. The activities and the questions in different lessons of the textbooks are designed for both genders.

In the context of Maldives the Social Studies textbooks, especially of Grade 6, for the first time in the whole of SAARC region, makes a mention of similarities of words in Sanskrit, Dhivehi and English. This similarity is mentioned in the following table—

Table 2.1 : Commonality of Words of the Week in Different Languages

Dhivehi	*Sanskrit*	*English*	*Name*
Aadheeththa	Aaadhiththa	Sunday	Sun
Hoama	Soama	Monday	Moon
Angaara	Angaahara	Tuesday	Mars
Budha	Budha	Wednesday	Mercury
Buraasfathi	Brihaspathi	Thursday	Jupiter
Hukuru	Sukra	Friday	Venus
Honihiru	Sani	Saturday	Saturn

Source: Social Studies I, Grade 6, p. 4, Education Development Centre, Male.

In connection with peace, conflict management and social tensions, the textbooks focus more on human activities in relation to nature. The books mention the gradual erosion of natural resources the world over as a result of growing consumerism and rising population. This phenomenon has resulted in the rising greenhouse effect. In the context of Maldives there is a mention of some factors effecting the fragile environment of Male in particular. They are a growing population due to migration of people from different Islands to the capital city. These twin factors have resulted in aggravating environment degradation in Male.

There is also a reference to growing salinity of underground water, problems related to garbage disposal, congestion and overcrowding of living spaces, vehicular pollution and the spread of contagious diseases due to over-crowding of migratory population from Islands to Male. There is a mention of the impact of migration on the different Islands of Maldives. In the context of women it has led to a virtual extinction of the traditional crafts and has also led to the growing phenomena of women headed households. Women in Island have now to face multiple responsibilities of looking after their children and fending for their families. Psychologically it has led to escalating social and emotional problems among the young and adolescent children who grow up devoid of parental love and affection. Steps for addressing these social problems by the government are stated in a very brief manner.

Besides environment the other crucial conflicting site, mentioned in the textbooks, is related to family as a primary agent of socialisation. There is a mention of the growing rate of divorces in Maldives and its impacts in eroding the delicate fabric of family ties and bonding with siblings. This social malaise affects the emotional stability of children belonging to different age groups. For managing this important social problem, the Social Studies textbooks make a very partial reference to certain steps taken by the government to address it. They are the enactment of family laws that regulate marriage and divorce, parenthood and guardianship. However, live examples or successful cases as a result of enactment of this law are not stated.

Reference to different contemporary conflicts due to multifarious reasons at the national and international levels is also mentioned. Historical reasons have been given in a very brief manner. Themes connected with this issue relate to Nationalism in Asia. The two World Wars, the cold war and the growing threat of nuclear wars etc. are stated in limited way. Different peace initiatives, for addressing these conflicts in the historical context and in the contemporary times are very mechanically stated. In this connection the non-violence technique of Mahatma Gandhi is mentioned very briefly. It is interesting to note that in classroom observations these themes were handled by teachers very mechanically. The pedagogical processes did not facilitate in arousing pupils' sensitivity in understanding the spirit that has guided the formulation of different peace initiatives the world over.

While some of the strategies for conflict resolution are not very apparent in textual and contextual situations, peace as a value finds a lot of space in the Social Studies textbooks. There is a mention of Islam having inbuilt human values of peace, mercy, generosity, forgiveness, modesty, happiness, negating all forms of violence and oppression, and promoting universal brotherhood. It is further stated that these intrinsic values embedded in Islam have succeeded in bringing people and societies together all over the world.

Besides evaluation of textual material, discussions were also held with teachers and students in all co-educational government schools in Male and in seven Island schools of four Atolls, namely Baa, Noonu, Lhaviyani and Gaafu Alifu. In these schools teachers and students were of the opinion that some of the content areas that needed to be detailed and few issues that need to be included for strengthening the component of gender with sensitivity towards peace are—

- inclusion of women role models, continuity and change regarding the status of women, indicators on the status of women in the society

- life and condition of the people of the atolls
- details about Maldivian history
- role of SAARC and other regional and international alliances in the context of learning to live together, culture and tradition of Maldivian society
- conservation and preservation of environment and biography of national leaders of Asia.

Thus, from the analysis of textual materials of the Republic of Maldives it appears that priority is given to strengthening national identity; gender and peace are woven into textbooks. In depth examination of textual materials in Social Studies, Environmental Studies and English, from the perspectives of gender and peace, highlights some positive strands. Women and men are shown in productive and active roles. The language used in the textual materials is gender inclusive and visuals depict both sexes in all activities related to education, economy and polity. Leadership qualities are associated with both sexes. Further, themes that discuss only men and women's contributions are done in context specific situations. However, despite weaving gender issues, books do have a tinge of stereotyping. Ascribed and socially constructed tailor made masculine and feminine roles for men and women are stated in a few themes. Generally, domestic chores are shown as women's primary roles and responsibility and income generating work for men.

In fact, stereotyping is visible in most of the textual materials of South Asian countries such as Pakistan, Nepal and Bangladesh.

It is interesting to note that from a comparative analysis of textbooks of neighbouring countries, the Maldivian textbooks, particularly in the domain of Social Studies, are way ahead. Social Studies textbooks of Pakistan, Bangladesh and Nepal, in the context of gender, adopt an add women and stir approach, whereas the Maldivian books treat gender in an integrated manner. Textbooks of Bangladesh, in the context of gender, adopt instrumentalist approach. Women's education is seen as critical for fertility control.

The only textbooks that are perhaps way ahead of Maldives and in SAARC region, that substantially weave gender concern's in selection of themes, content and visual portrayal, are textbooks prepared by government agency in India. The National Council of Educational Research and Training (NCERT) is a nodal agency that prepares textbooks for school children at all levels. All the textbooks based on NCF-2005, particularly in the domain of Social Studies, Languages and Environmental Studies, have addressed gender issues both in the content and visual portrayal. The backs of cover pages, inward facing, in all books have small visuals and slogans for promoting girls' education. A special feature of the textbooks is that they have captured the voices of marginalised sections of the society and have tried to incorporate the rich diversity of the cultural heritage. Poignant case studies of discrimination are also referred in some books. Effort has been made to make books child friendly by adopting the constructivist approach.

In the context of peace the authors of the above-mentioned countries portray peace more as a human value. Conflict management strategies of addressing emerging social issues in connection with environment and society are missing and are given very low priority in textual materials. Skills of peace building are nearly absent in all textbooks of Pakistan, Bangladesh, Nepal and Maldives.

The next chapter throws light on the dynamics of schooling processes in the Republic in the context of gender and peace.

REFERENCES

1. Arnot, Madeleine. 2006. *Gender Voices in the Classroom,* Cambridge University (talk on 23rd November, 2006) at University of Delhi.
2. Hayward, Ruth Finney. 2000. *Breaking the Earthenware Jar: Lessons from South Asia to End Violence against Women,* UNICEF.
3. Srivastava, Gouri. 2005. *Gender Concerns in the Social Studies Textbooks of Pakistan and Bangladesh,* International Textbook Research, Braunschweig, Germany.

4. Srivastava, Gouri. 2006. *Envisioning the Common Historical and Cultural Past, Gender Concerns and Conflict Management and Social Tensions: An Analysis of Upper Primary Textbooks of Social Studies Textbooks of Pakistan, Bangladesh and Nepal,* Social Change, Vol. 36. No. 2.
5. Tawil, Sobhi and Harley, Alexandra, 2004. *Education, Conflict and Social Cohesion,* International Bureau of Education, UNESCO, Geneva.

ENGLISH CORE READERS : GRADE 1

1. Athif, Mun-ish, *What's That Sound,* Male, EDC {Educational Development Centre}, 2005, p. 12.
2. Nadiya, Fathimath, *My Baby Brother,* Male, EDC, 2005, p. 12.
3. Nadiya, Fathimath, *Sha's Birthday,* Male, EDC, 2005, p. 12.
4. Nadiya, Fathimath, *Mirza went Shopping,* Male, EDC, 2005, p. 12.
5. Nadiya, Fathimath, *Animal Friends,* Male, EDC, 2005, p. 12.
6. Nadiya, Fathimath, *Eid,* Male, EDC, p. 12.
7. Nadiya, Fathimath, *Going Fishing,* Male, EDC, 2005, p. 12.
8. Nadiya, Fathimath, *Mango Baby,* Male, EDC, 2005, p. 12.
9. Nadiya, Fathimath, *The Lost Kitten,* Male, EDC, 2005, p. 12.
10. Nadiya, Fathimath, *A Farm in My House,* Male, EDC, 2005, p. 12.
11. Nadiya, Fathimath, *The Look Alike Houses,* Male, EDC, 2005, p. 12.
12. Nadiya, Fathimath, *Rima's Day,* Male, EDC, 2005, p. 12.
13. Nadiya, Fathimath, *Gardening,* Male, EDC, 2005, p. 12.
14. Nadiya, Fathimath, *A Rainy Day,* Male, EDC, 2005, p. 12.
15. Nadiya, Fathimath, *A Week from My Diary,* Male, EDC, 2005, p. 12.
16. Nadiya, Fathimath, *Bubbles,* Male, EDC, 2005, p. 12.
17. Nadiya, Fathimath, *Water,* Male, EDC, 2005, p. 12.
18. Nadiya, Fathimath, *Is Rashid Sick?* Male, EDC, 2005, p. 12.
19. Nadiya, Fathimath, *Shafa's School,* Male, EDC, 2005, p. 12.
20. Nadiya, Fathimath, *Daddy is Late for Work,* Male, EDC, 2005, p. 12.
21. Nadiya, Fathimath, *Magic,* Male, EDC, 2005, p. 12.
22. Nadiya, Fathimath, *What Comes from a Coconut Tree,* Male, EDC, 2005, p. 12.
23. Nadiya, Fathimath, *Brown Bear,* Male, EDC, 2005, p. 13.
24. Nadiya, Fathimath, *Fazal's Lace,* Male, EDC, 2005, p. 12.
25. Nadiya, Fathimath, *Hobby,* Male, EDC, 2005, p. 12.
26. Nadiya, Fathimath, *Presents from the Island,* Male, EDC, 2005, p. 12.
27. Nadiya, Fathimath, *What a Mess,* Male, EDC, 2005, p. 12.
28. Nadiya, Fathimath, *The Nut,* Male, EDC, 2005, p. 12.
29. Nadiya, Fathimath, *The Baby Sitter,* Male, EDC, 2005, p. 12.
30. Nadiya, Fathimath, *On the Island,* Male, EDC, 2005, p. 12.
31. Shahuma, Mariyam, *I Want to Play,* Male, EDC, 2005, p. 12.

32. Shakeel, Hubasha, *Out in the Garden*, Male, EDC, 2005, p. 9.
33. Shakeel, Hubasha, *Ely's Fun Day at the Beach*, Male, EDC, 2005, p. 9.
34. Yakshan, Abdulla, *Molly the Lazy Fish*, Male, EDC, 2005, p. 11.

GRADE 2

35. Gobey, Mary, *English Core Reader: Grade 2, Book 1*, Male, Impress Print, 2005, p. 36.
36. Gobey, Mary, *English Core Reader: Grade 2, Book 2*, Male, Impress Print, 2003, p. 36.
37. Gobey, Mary, *English Core Reader: Grade 2, Book 3*, Male, Impress Print, 2005, p. 33.
38. Gobey, Mary, *English Core Reader: Grade 2, Book 4*, Male, Million Book Shop, 2006, p. 35.
39. Gobey, Mary, *English Core Reader: Grade 2, Book 5*, Male, Srinivas Fine Arts, 2004, p. 43.
40. Bell, Lorraine, Khaleel, Mariyam, *English Core Reader: Grade 3, Book 1*, Male, Impress Print, 2003, p. 19.

GRADE 3

41. Bell, Lorraine, Khaleel, Mariyam, *English Core Reader: Grade 3 Book2*, Male, Aaraha Service, 2007, p. 31.
42. Bell, Lorraine, Khaleel, Mariyam, *English Core Reader: Grade 3, Book 3*, Male, Karaanee Printer and Publisher, 2006, p. 23.
43. Bell, Lorraine, Khaleel, Mariyam, *English Core Reader: Grade 3, Book 4*, Male, Impress Print, 2005, p. 23.
44. Bell, Lorraine, Khaleel, Mariyam, *English Core Reader: Grade 3, Book 5*, Male, Impress Print, 2005, p. 22.

GRADE 4

45. Bell, Lorraine, Khaleel, Mariyam, *English Core Reader: Grade 4, Book 1*, Male, Impress Print, 2003, p. 14.
46. Bell, Lorraine, Khaleel, Mariyam, *English Core Reader: Grade 4, Book 2*, Male, Impress Print, 2003, p. 18.
47. Bell, Lorraine, Khaleel, Mariyam, *English Core Reader: Grade 4, Book 3*, Male, Impress Print, 2005, p. 28.
48. Bell, Lorraine, Khaleel, Mariyam, *English Core Reader: Grade 4, Book 4*, Male, Faseyha Press, 2003, p. 22.
49. Bell, Lorraine, Khaleel, Mariyam, *English Core Reader: Grade 4, Book 5*, Male, Faseyha Press, 2003, p. 26.

GRADE 5

50. Gasim, Kathma, *English Core Reader, Grade 5, Book 1*, India, Lovely Offset Printer, 2005, p. 40.
51. Gasim, Kathma, *English Core Reader, Grade 5, Book 2*, India, Lovely Offset Printers, 2005, p. 42.

GRADE 6

52. Khaleel, Mariyam, *English Core Reader, Grade 6*, Male, Litho Print, 2007, p. 116.

GRADE 7

53. Khaleel, Mariyam, *English Core Reader: Grade7*, Male, Atoll Market Pvt. Limited, 2006, p. 126.

ENGLISH PUPIL'S BOOK, GRADE 1—7

54. Nadia, Fathimath, *English For Us, 1A, 1B*, India, Blue Bird, 2006, p. 88.
55. Gobey, Mary, *The New English: Grade 2, Pupil's Book*, India, Lovely Offset Printers, 2006, p. 178.
56. Bell, Lorraine, Khaleel, Mariyam, *The New English: Grade 3 Pupils Book*, Male, Aaraha Service, 2007, p. 156.
57. Bell, Lorraine, Khaleel, Mariyam, *The New English: Grade 4, Pupils Book*, India, Lovely Offset Printers, 2007, p. 151.
58. Bell, Lorraine, Khaleel, Mariyam, *The New English: Grade 5, Pupils Book*, India, Lovely Offset Printers, 2007, p. 154.
59. Hartley, Julia, *The New English Grade 6, Pupils Book*, Male, Asrafee Book Shop, 2007, p. 271.
60. Ali, Aminath, Mohamed, Naashia, *English 7: Students Book*, Male, Atoll Market, Pvt. Ltd., 2007, p. 226.

ENVIRONMENTAL STUDIES, GRADE 1—5

61. Shakir, Fathimath, Nahid, *Environmental Studies 1*, Male, Lovely Offset Printer, India, 2007, p. 142.
62. Shakir, Fathimath, Nahid, *Environmental Studies 2*, Male, Lovely Offset Printers, India, 2007, p. 126.
63. Ismail, Aminath, Samad, Arif, Abdul, *Environmental Studies*, 3A, Male, Litho Print, 2007, p. 126.
64. Shakeeb, Ahmed, Shakir, Nahid, *Environmental Studies*, Grade 4, Pupils Book, India, Lovely Offset Printers, 2007, p. 114.

65. Shakeeb, Ahmed, Shakir, *Environmental Studies,* Grade 5, Pupils Book, India, Lovely Offset Printers, 2005, p. 114.

SOCIAL STUDIES, GRADE 6—7

66. Ahmed, Mariyam, Azra, Siciliano, Pamela, *Social Studies 1, Grade 6,* Male, Atoll, Market Pvt. Ltd. 2007, p. 114.
67. Ahmed, Mariyam, Azra, Waheed, Muhammad, Muhammed, Ahmed, Gafoor, Abdul, Adam, Khadeeja, Hameed, Shaheen, *Social Studies 2, Grade 7,* Sivakasi, India, The Orient Processor, 2003, p. 86.

UNPUBLISHED PAPERS AND REPORTS

68. Yashi, Ahmed, Nashid, Hassan, Nahid, Fathimath, 2007. *Gender Analysis of Primary Textbooks,* Male.
69. *Social Studies, Grades 6 and 7, Syllabus,* 1990. Educational Development Centre, Male, p. 110.
70. *Environmental Studies, Syllabus,* 1990. Educational Development Centre, Male, p. 15.
71. *The Draft Syllabus for English in the National Curriculum,* 2004. Educational Development Centre, Male, p. 146.
72. *The Framework of the National Curriculum, Draft of Unofficial Translation,* 1999. Educational Development Centre, Male, p. 10.

3

Conformity and Contestation

A Study of Schooling Processes in the Republic of Maldives

The destiny of a nation takes shape in the classrooms. The art of teaching has a deep imprint in crafting of personalities. Schooling and classroom processes helps in transacting learning to do, learning to be, learning to know and learning to live together.

The Republic of Maldives has the credit of providing schooling facilities to all children of the school going age. As an important secondary agent of socialisation, the mini society influences children in their overall personality development. In the formulation of gender identities they either help in strengthening masculine or feminine traits or attempt to demystify them. Studies in the context of South Asia and Commonwealth countries by Kirk (2005), Page and Jha (2009), have shown that schooling processes strengthen masculine and feminine roles, tailor-made for boys and girls. They hardly generate processes that bring about transformatory changes. In other words schools replicate prevalent values and norms in the society and thereby maintain *status quo*.

In the context of peace, studies Page and Jha (2009) and Srivastava (1997), have shown that schools, especially managed by government agency and those receiving aid, either strengthen peace as a value or create conditions at times when conflicts regarding behavioural issues are settled through

Source: Thajuddin School, Male and Fareediyya School, Hulhumale.

consensus or negotiation. Researches have shown that the world over schools adopt long term or short term strategies for integrating peace in the content and process of education. Short term peace goals focus more on reformative and curative aspects by adopting peace keeping strategies. The long term goal of making children acquire skills of gender harmony, and peace building relations that include skills of negotiation and consensus, are very often ignored or given low priority.

In the present chapter the focus is on examining the dynamics of gender and peace in the schooling and classroom processes in the Republic of Maldives. In 2005 the total number of schools in the Republic was approximately 214 and in 2007 it was 232. Schools in Maldives can be categorised into three broad categories, i.e. the Government managed, Ward/ Community and Private schools. Although education is largely provided by the government, the community and the private sector also play an active role. The government supports community and private schools by providing a certain percentage of teachers, depending on the school size, and by providing infrastructure facilities and financial subsidies. In order to minimise the differences in giving provisions to schools, 135 community schools in the Atolls were converted to government schools in 2005.

In the capital city Male, formal school is preceded by two years pre-primary education in the lower and upper kindergarten. This form of pre-primary education is now increasing in the Atolls, especially in the highly populated Islands. The alternative to this form of education is the *Edhuruge (traditional educational centre)* based in the house of a learned person. Modern pre-school and traditional *Edhuruge* provide the first organised learning opportunity for 90% of pre-school children.

Primary education of children begins at the age of six at which children enter a seven year cycle, starting in Grade 1 and ending in Grade 7. As mentioned earlier universalising seven years of basic education was one of the landmark achievements of the country. Presently the net Enrolment Ratio for the first seven years of basic education stands at 100%. The Assessment in these grades is at school level, on the basis of continuous assessment in grades 1 to 3, and school based examination held three times a year in grades 4 to 7.

Secondary education in Maldives consists of grades 8-10 (lower secondary) and grades 11-12 (higher secondary). Initially Secondary education was provided only in Male until 1990, but has been extended to the Atolls through the gradual addition of grades 8-10 in some Atoll Education Centres and Atoll Schools' on set criteria, and by the establishment of two regional secondary schools. In 2005, the criterion for introducing Grade 8 in the existing primary schools was revised so that more students could get easy access to 10 years of formal schooling.

Introduction of Higher Secondary Schooling in the Atolls began initially in two Atolls in 2001, followed by another one in 2002. Further expansion of the opportunity for providing higher secondary education in the Atolls continued by establishing Grade 11 in 10 eligible existing secondary schools in 2004 and by establishing another four schools in 2005 and six in 2006. One higher secondary school had to be closed due to unavailability of eligible students. Hence, altogether 24 schools are offering higher secondary education across the country.

Examination System in the Republic

School examinations are held three times a year, at the end of grades 10 and 12. Students are expected to sit for the

International General Certificate of Secondary Education (IGCSE), General Certificate of Education (GCE) Ordinary Level examinations and GCE Advanced Level examination of the Cambridge International Examination (CIE) or the London Examination, Edexcel International. National assessment is based on the results of these examinations. Since October 2002, almost all students from the secondary schools have been sitting in the IGCSE and GCE O/L syllabuses of the Cambridge International Examinations. In 2005, 142 centres (including both school and private centres) entered the October/November sessions of the CIE examinations out of the 156 centres registered at CIE.

Medium of Education

The medium of education in all schools in the Republic is English. The shift from the spoken language, i.e. Dhivehi to English medium could be due to growing consumerism and linkage of Maldives with international countries. Growing tourism and its reliance on foreign trade especially in basic food items, and expatriate labour force have necessitated enhancing the demand for English as a medium of spoken and written language.

An alternative to the national English medium education is offered by Arabic medium. *Madhrasthul Arabiyyathul Islaamiyya* offers preparatory level classes and the *Kulliyyathul Dhiraasaathil Islaamiyya* offers secondary as well as higher secondary level classes. In addition to these two government schools, both of which are in Male, *Madhrasathul Islamiyya* in S. Hithadhoo also offer Arabic as a curriculum subject.

Table 3.1 depicts slight variation in enrolment of boys and girls in the Republic at different levels of education. Perhaps this could be due to the difference in the population of boys and girls in the Republic. This trend in enrolment was also visible in 2007 when the present study was undertaken.

Table 3.1 : Enrolment of Children in different types of schools in the Republic

Locality	Type	Level					Total
		Pre-Primary	Primary	Lower Primary	Higher Secon-dry	Special Classes	
Male	Government	113	12397	5581	1372	101	19564
	Community	4025	936	2146	0	0	7107
	Private	430	541	2289	105	0	3365
	Total	***4568***	***13874***	***10016***	***1477***	***101***	***30036***
Atolls	Government	1490	43698	18340	465	6	63999
	Community	2738	0	0	0	0	2738
	Private	4709	301	290	0	0	5300
	Total	***8937***	***43999***	***18630***	***465***	***6***	***72037***
Republic	***Total***	***13505***	***57873***	***28646***	***1942***	***107***	***102073***

In Male at the pre-primary level, in 2005 community school enrolled large number of children as compared to government and private schools. However, at the primary level a reverse trend was observed. More children were enrolled in government schools as compared to community and private schools. At the Higher Secondary stage government initiative surpassed those of private. Education of the specially challenged was fully managed by the government.

Source: School Statistics, 2005, Ministry of Education.

Table 3.2 : Enrolment of Children by Levels

Level	Both Sexes	Boys (%)	Girls (%)
Pre-Primary	13,505	6,894 **(51)**	6,611 **(49)**
Primary (1-7)	57,873	30,206 **(52.2)**	27,667 **(47.8)**
Lower Secondary (8-10)	28,646	13,673 **(47.7)**	14,973 **(52.3)**
Higher Secondary (11-12)	1,942	1,026 **(52.8)**	916 **(47.2)**
Special Classes	107	53 **(49.5)**	54 **(50.5)**
Total	102,073	51,852**(50.8)**	50,221**(49.2)**

Source: Statistical Yearbook of Maldives, 2006, p. 81 (Figures in the brackets are percentages).

The above information on enrolments was acquired during fieldwork conducted in 2007. From the above two tables (3.1 and 3.2) it appears that there is minor difference in enrolments between the two sexes. In 2006, the enrolment of boys was 50.8% and for the girls it was 49.2%. In 2007 it was 50.7% for boys and 49.3% for girls in schools that were visited.

This slight difference in enrolments between sexes could be due to the difference in the population of males and females, as mentioned earlier. In 2006, the population of males in the Republic was 151,796 and that of the females was 147,073. Besides, this, some other factors could have contributed to this phenomenon such as migration of families from Islands to Male. Another factor that could have impacted school enrolments could be the migration of students between schools in Male. This could have led to fluctuations in enrolment between schools. The movement of population between Islands and Male had increased especially after the Tsunami in 2004. Another possibility could be the urbanisation of Male, and the immense opportunity it offered in the past and the present in the context of offering better educational and professional opportunities to its people of different age groups.

Thus, despite overcrowding of Male, one can deduce from the enrolment figures that Maldives is very close to the Millennium Development Goals (MDG). This fact was substantiated in 2007, when field visits were conducted in 17 schools in Male and 6 in four Atolls, namely Noonu, Lhaviyani, Baa and Gaafu Alifu. In all schooling and classroom observations it was found that they were sites of conformity as well as contestation.

Table 3.3 : Enrolment of boys and girls in Male and Atolls in 2007

Name of the School	*Year of foundation*	*Grades*	*Boys (%)*	*Girls (%)*	*Total*
Government Primary and Secondary Schools in Male					
Ghiyasuddin	1999	1-7	1039 **(50.5)**	1018 **(49.5)**	2057
Imaduddin	2000	1-7	994 **(52)**	918 **(48.0)**	1912
Iskandhar	1961	1-7	1252 **(51.1)**	1197 **(48.9)**	2449
Jamaluddin	1985	1-7	976 **(49.6)**	993 **(50.4)**	1969
Kalafaafannu	1989	1-7	780 **(50.4)**	767 **(49.6)**	1547
Thaajuddin	1989	1-7	911 **(50.6)**	890 **(49.4)**	1801
A.A. Islamiyya	1987	1-7	195 **(51)**	186 **(49)**	381
Muhyiddin	1994	1-9	406 **(53)**	360 **(47)**	766
Fareedhiyya	2004	1-10	357 **(54)**	307 **(46)**	664
Aminiya School	1944	8-10		2502 **(100)**	2502
Majeedhiya	1951	8-10	1328 **(100)**	—	1328
Dharumavantha School	2002	8-10	1274 **(100)**	—	1274

(contd.)

Table 3.3 (Contd.)

Name of the School	Year of foundation	Grades	Boys (%)	Girls (%)	Total
		Ward/Private Schools in Male			
Madhrasathul Ameer Ahmed	1984	7-10	220 **(55)**	180 **(45)**	400
Madhrasathul Ahmadhiya	1982	6-10	506 **(40.9)**	732 **(59.1)**	1238
Madhrasathul Aliya	1965	5-10	31 **(53.4)**	27 **(46.6)**	58
Galholhu Madharusa	1984	8-10	159 **(44)**	202 **(59)**	361
Maafannu Madharusa	1984	6-10	133 **(44.8)**	164 **(55.2)**	297
		Island Schools in some Atolls			
Fohdhoo	**1972**	1-7	18 **(45)**	22 **(55)**	40
Kudafaree Madhrasa	**1969**	1-10	65 **(50.8)**	63 **(49.2)**	128
Hidhaayaa	**1980**	1-10	163 **(55.8)**	129 **(44.2)**	292
Madhrasa Ifthithaan Naifaru	**1933**	1-12	521 **(52.2)**	476 **(47.7)**	998
Baa Atoll Educational Centre	**1978**	1-12	517 **(55.5)**	415 **(44.5)**	932
Thulhaadhoo School	**1947**	1-12	246 **(54.8)**	203 **(45.2)**	449
Gaafu Alifu Atoll	**1981**	1-12	375 **(54.3)**	**315** **(45.7)**	690

Source: Details of School visits conducted in 2007 (Figures in the brackets are percentages).

Infrastructure Facilities in the Schools in Maldives

All schools in Male and in the islands are well endowed in terms of physical facilities such as proper ventilated rooms, furniture, blackboards, library, playgrounds, drinking water, prayer room, computer labs, and separate toilets for boys and girls and supervisors room of varying size. These basic facilities were available in Male and in other islands. However, facilities of science labs and availability of reference books related to Science and Social Sciences was wanting in Male schools and in the Atoll schools. In all schools that were visited veiling was observed by a few girl students. It is interesting to note that the whiteness of the uniform of children in schools that used white colour was visible throughout the day. The environment of all schools in Male and in the Islands was very clean and neat. Schools in the Republic have been named after the Sultans of Maldives.

Curriculum plus activity in Island School

Source: Madhrasa Ifthithaah Naifaru.

A joyful event in the School

Source: Muhyiddin School.

Vision Statement

All schools focus on translating the vision of the nation into practice. The vision statement stresses on the promotion of religious and cultural values among the Maldivian students that would help in fostering social cohesion among them and enable them to nurture patriotic feelings towards their country. It is also envisioned that education would help in providing children with necessary knowledge and skills so that children who go through the Maldivian system of education are skilled to be productive, and are able and active participants in the national and international arena.

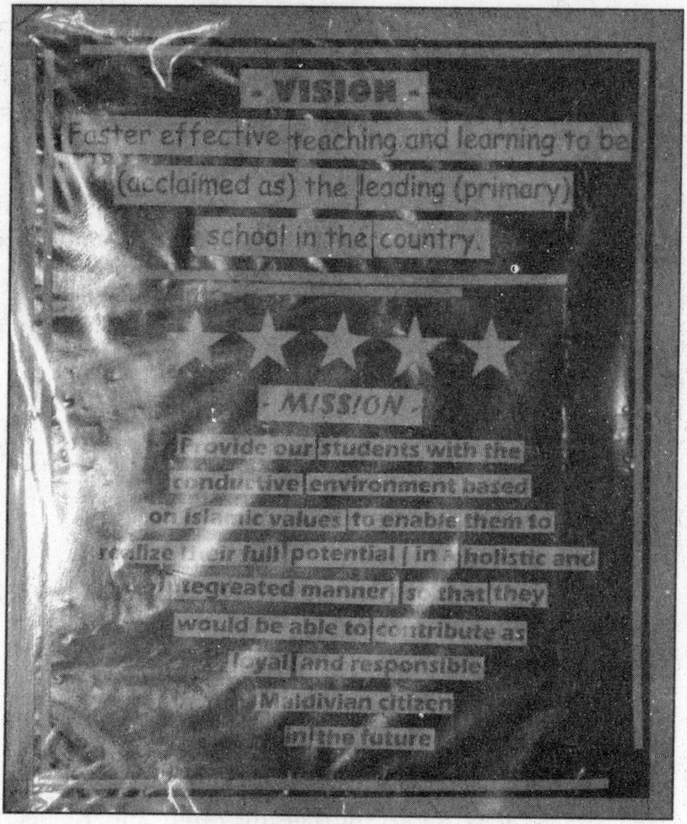

Vision and Mission statement

Source: Imaduddin School.

During the course of field visits to different categories of schools in Male and in the Atolls it was found that all schools conform to the philosophy embedded in the vision statement of the government. In the context of school organisation in Maldives it was found that human values were depicted outside and inside the classrooms. Some of them are mentioned below—

Character is like a tree and reputation is like a shadow. The shadow is what we think of it; the tree is the real thing.

(***Abraham Lincoln,*** mentioned in Fareedhiyya School, Hulhumale)

Watch your Thoughts they become Words
Watch your Words, they become Actions
Watch your Actions, they become Habits
Watch your Habits, they become Character
Watch your Character, it becomes your Destiny.

(Jamaluddin School, Male)

Some of the classrooms had captions on the wall portraying the code of conduct that was expected from the pupils, such as—

Talk politely to everyone.
Be Punctual.
Use the Dustbin.
Do not disturb the class.
Do not scribble on the wall or on the desk.
Say 'excuse me please' before you enter.
Complete your home work.
Keep your bags on the floor.

(Quotes in classroom in Jamaluddin School, Male)

The focus of values mentioned within schools and in outside spaces was on strengthening open and respectful attitudes towards principals, teachers, students, managers, supervisors, staff involved in cleaning etc. Focus of the vision statement was strengthening the bonding between student and staff, and resolving all kinds of conflict through consensus and negotiation. Promoting fair rules applicable to both sexes, encouraging inclusive activities related to peace, openness, compassion and empathy for all, and equality of opportunity for boys and girls was also emphasised upon.

Assemblies held in schools that were visited ensured participation of all children. School songs that were sung in Maldivian Schools laid stress on inculcating among children, love and pride for their nation. The translated version of the school song sung in all schools is as follows—

> *Let's study happily when we are young and beautify ourselves with good etiquettes.*
> *Let's also educate and discipline ourselves according to the way our forefathers have done and in such a way that we obey our beloved nation/government.*
> *Let's also be ready to provide good service for the sake of our religions and nation and become citizens having real Maldivian Blood.*

(***School Song*** translated by Shafeega, Student at the Maldives College of Higher Education, Male)

Sites of conformity are also visible in Teachers Handbook, Students Handbook, School Magazines and Year Planners that were readily available in all schools that were visited. Some of the glimpses of expected code of conduct stated in the handbook are mentioned below—

School Rules

Students must abide by and adhere to the principles of Islam.

Students should obey and respect the Principal, Supervisors, Teachers and Office Staff.

Every student must work to their best and strive for the highest.

Students must respect and talk to their elders politely.

Students must be courteous and be helpful at all times.

Students should be punctual to school sessions and other activities.

Students should come dressed neatly and properly to school.

No jewellery is allowed other than simple ear studs on girls.

(Students Handbook 2004, Iskandhar School, Male)

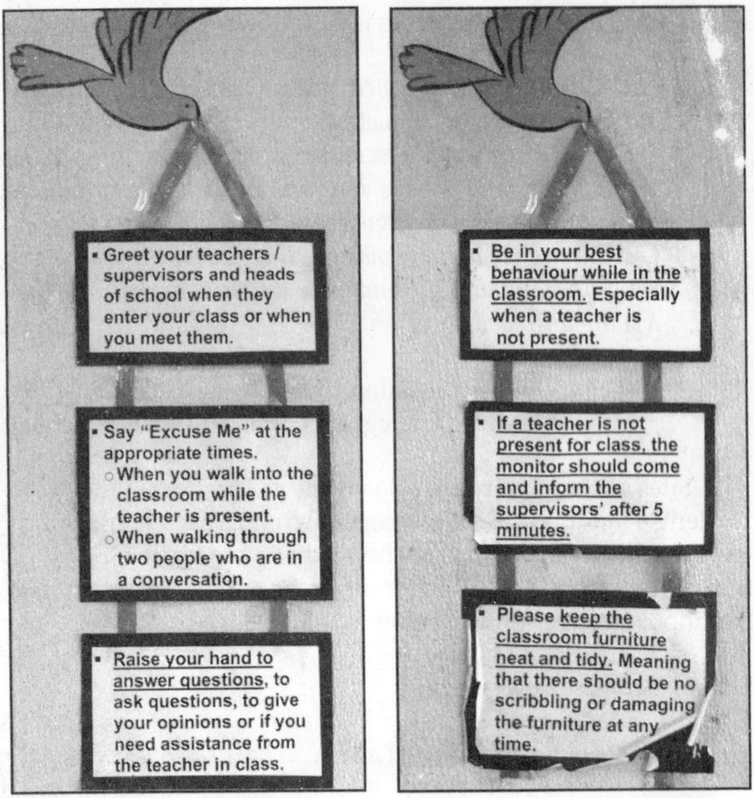

A portrayal of code of conduct for students

Source: Kalaafaanu School.

It is interesting to note that along with conformity, principles of gender inclusive approach were followed in the schooling processes in the Republic. This phenomenon also conforms to the social milieu. Girls and boys are treated equally by parents and equal opportunities are provided to them in education, a phenomena that was existing in the past and continues till date. School observation also confirmed this. Some of the visible sites of equity and equality were witnessed in the recitation of the Holy Quran. Boys and girls were given alternate chances to read passages from this Holy Scripture. In Baa Atoll Educational Centre, the entrance of the school had a list of achievers that included the names of boys and girls who had excelled academically and were all-rounders in curriculum plus activities, such as sports, debates, recitations and dramatics.

Picture of Achievers

Baa Atoll Educational Centre

Further, schooling processes also encouraged children who were mildly challenged to participate in all curriculum plus activities.

In physical education classes children of both sexes participate. It is interesting to note that even though football is a popular sport among boys and badminton and volleyball among girls, in Kalafaafannu school, football was jointly played by boys and girls.

Happy integration of children with special needs

Source: Imaduddin School, Male.

Gender inclusive sport activities

Source: Kalafaafannu School, Male.

In Jamaluddin, Kalafaafannu, Ghiyasuddin and Thaajuddin schools, children wore same uniform in physical education classes. Overall schooling processes were highly controlled and monitored by different cadres of functionaries such as Principal, Deputy Principal, Senior Assistant Principals and Supervisors for each grade. The supervisors, as the word denotes, meticulously ensured that children as well as teachers conformed to school rules and regulations, and that discipline was maintained at all costs. Every school had a separate room for supervisors which was air-conditioned. All supervisors were Maldivians. Thus Maldivian schooling processes overtly reflected a high degree of conformity.

Some curriculum plus activities

Source: Kudafaree Madhrasa.

Reflection of Classroom Processes

Observations

The total number of classroom observations conducted was 87 in primary grades (1 to 7) and lower secondary grades (8 to 10). Generally three classes were observed per school. In few schools additional classes were observed, e.g. In Muhyiddin School four classes were observed and in Madhrasathul Ifthithaah and in Baa Atoll Educational Centre 12 classes were observed. Classroom observations were limited to the content areas related to the domain of English, Social Studies and Environmental Studies at the primary grades. In secondary grades, classes that were observed related to the disciplinary areas of History, Geography, Economics and English.

Glimpses of gender inclusive classroom processes

Source: Kalafaafannu School, Male.

Teaching and Learning

The student teacher ratio varied from school to school. It was between 1:30 and 1:34 in a few schools in Male. Spaces in classrooms were sufficient for the teachers and students to move freely without jostling and pushing. In all classes that were observed nearly all teachers, male and female, were constantly moving while teaching. Teachers' movement ensured the following—

- Strengthened conformity and obedience among students

- Ensured children were attentive
- Teacher's eye contact and body language attempted to ensure discouragement of all kinds of deviant activities that would perhaps lead to anomalous situations
- Helped teachers to know whether content delivery helped in making the children understand difficult concepts
- Facilitating students in conducting activities
- Motivating peer interactions.

Pedagogical Processes

In the context of pedagogy, in all classes that were observed, the initial 10 to 15 minutes were teacher centred. The remaining time was utilised in the adoption of different participatory techniques such as group work, pair work, quiz, riddles, puzzles and games that ensured gender responsive pedagogical processes. It is significant to note that boys and girls participated equally in classes. However, it was limited to a few children. In the lower secondary grades boys were more vocal than girls in questioning and getting their doubts cleared, answering questions and in providing additional information in connection with the lesson that was taught. In primary classes girls took the lead. An interesting aspect of classroom processes was the peer group interactions. It was visible in all participatory techniques that were adopted by the teachers and was visible in the exchange of stationary items, getting doubts cleared, eating together in intervals and in practising music, dance and sports.

Classroom Management

In the context of classroom management there appeared distinct patterns in the sitting arrangements. In grades 5 to 6 the sitting was mixed in government schools.

Sitting pattern became segregated from grades seven onwards in government, ward and private schools.

Mixed sitting and gender inclusive classroom activities

Source: Madhrasa Ifthithaah Naifaru.

Classroom portraying that veiling was not compulsory

Source: Madhrasathul Ahmadhiya.

Few classes in ward schools in grades seven and eight were mixed because of shortage of teachers in Science and Maths. However, in Almadharasathul Arabiyathul Islamiyya and other Ward Schools in Male, though schools were co-educational, classes of boys and girls were held separately.

School song sung by boys and girls

Source: Jamaluddin School, Male.

Roles and Responsibilities

Roles and responsibilities were evenly distributed among boys and girls. In a discussion held with teachers, principals and students, it was mentioned that activities inside classrooms such as cleaning the blackboard, bringing chalk, duster, teaching and learning materials, collection of assignments and other miscellaneous activities were jointly performed by both sexes. Similarly in the context of roles, effort was made by schools to demystify tailor made masculine and feminine roles prescribed by the society for boys and girls. Principals and teachers constantly worked towards instilling leadership, decision-making and sharing of responsibilities in both sexes. Exposure to unconventional skills related to the use of computers was taught to boys and girls. Thus, every effort was made by schools to bring a gradual change in the status of children from ascribed to achieved status, whereby children would be judged not by particular standards but by universal ones, based solely on performance.

Schools and Classrooms as Sites of Contestation

During school visits and classroom observations, the classroom talk, subject talk and voices outside classrooms revealed that very often the mechanism adopted for making children conform to school rules led to simmering deviance in their behaviour patterns. This aspect was very visible in all schools. Another factor that led to schools becoming sites of contestation was the changing socio-economic and political scenario in the Republic. In the economic domain growing inflation rate coupled with the limited finance of the household, fewer employment opportunities, had a direct bearing on children and their education. Children, especially adolescents from low socio-economic background, had very defeatist attitude and were not interested in pursuing higher education or professional courses. They were mainly interested in earning money and helping their families. In discussions held with children in all schools, it was found that even though they had very high educational and occupational aspirations, children were not very sure about the courses they should opt for in future or the skills needed for pursuing them. Also, they were not clear about places where they could get employment. Most of the boys in Madhrasa Ifthithaah, Naifaru and Maafannu Madharusa belonging to Grade 7 appeared to be apathetic about what they wanted to take up as a profession in later life. In the former school some boys mentioned that they wanted to be fishermen and few were not sure what they wanted to be. Most of the children in Maafannu Madharusa at Male were not interested in their studies and had difficulty in coping with subjects such as English and Maths. The reason cited was that most of their outside school hours were spent in doing small jobs for sustaining themselves in Male.

Minor Conflicting Sites in Schools

Very often lack of motivation in studies led to behavioural problems such as disturbing peers in class, not responding to questions being asked by the teachers, not being attentive, laughing, throwing paper balls and using abusive language. Constant efforts were being made to address the above problems by adopting diagnostic, curative and reformatory approaches. In schools that had counselling facilities, the counsellor would attempt to address maladjusted children. During fieldwork, in all schools in Male and in the Atolls, deviance in behaviour by adolescent children was observed mainly in lower secondary grades. This was also true of single sex schools in Male.

In the social realm, the phenomena of intake of drugs by children, especially adolescents, had also led to escalation of conflicts and social tensions in schools. Children prone to taking drugs were not enthusiastic in their studies, appeared sleepy during classroom hours and lacked interest for understanding concepts that were taught in sciences and social sciences. Language of communication was very objectionable towards their peers and seniors. Attitude towards the teachers was also very hostile. Such behavioural problems were observed at some schools such as at Naifaru in lower secondary grades and were also reported by teachers and principals of different schools in Male such as Aminiya School and Maafannu Madharasa at Male.

Another social malice affecting the Republic was the phenomena of child abuse and divorces. These twin emerging social problems were very closely related to growing urbanisation and consumerism in the entire Republic. This had an impact on the emotional well being of children. Children from broken homes, and who were physically and emotionally abused faced problems of insecurity and alienation in schools. Very often children who were victims of this phenomena showed violent behavioural problems. Teachers reported that they were defiant and were not ready to adjust with their peers.

As mentioned earlier, schools adopted measures to address this problem. At times counsellors were active in solving problems of children who were maladjusted. Effort was also made by taking parents into confidence. Corporal punishment and stigmatising the child with behavioural problems were strictly prohibited.

Other possible contributing phenomena that made schooling and classroom processes a site of contestation was the growing political turmoil that impacted the overall schooling climate. Emergence of multi party system with different ideologies influenced a lot of adolescent children. This was witnessed in most of the schools and classroom observations conducted during 2007. Voices of the children within and outside classrooms showed that they wanted to change the symbols that were associated with government in power. These symbols related to the systematic control exercised by the school functionaries, schools rules and regulations that strengthened, conformity. In a discussion held with teachers and students they were of the view that the schooling processes did not help children acquire skills of self-reliance and overall development. Some of the children wanted to join politics to initiate changes that would link education with skills and overall personality development. In fact, they were looking forward to the forthcoming referendum to be held in 2007 and also the elections. (After 30 years, Maldives has now, in 2008, a new President, Mohammed Anni Nasheed of the Maldivian Democratic Party).

Thus, schooling processes in the Republic overtly and covertly reflect signs of conformity to Maldivian vision statement of envisioning a generation deeply committed to the Islamic values and love for the country. The changing socio-economic and political environment affecting the entire society, and the schooling processes in particular, shows growing signs of deviance and contestation.

The desire to bring change in existing scenario representing *status quo*, was simmering among the future voices of Maldives. This phenomena was witnessed during intensive fieldwork conducted in the Republic during April to December 2007.

The fourth chapter is about the Education of Women in Dhivehi Raajje in the past and the present.

Picture of Girls and Boys playing together

Source: Kalafaafannu School, Male.

REFERENCES

Bell, H.C.P., 1940. *op.cit.*

Cambridge Education: Strengthening the Framework of Education Towards Vision 2020, Draft Final Report, Prepared by Cambridge Education, 18 December, 2005.

Denham, Edward Brandis, Census of 1911, *The Maldives.*

Dias, Edward, 1949. *op.cit.*

Maloney, C. 1980. *People of the Maldives Island*, Orient Longman, New Delhi.

Srivastava, Gouri, 2007. *Gender and Peace: Educational Policy Curriculum, English, Environmental Studies, Social Studies Textbooks of the Republic of Maldives (unpublished report).*

4

Education of Women
Past and Present in Maldives

The crux of human resource development is ensuring education to all, irrespective of gender, class and location. The content and process of education should be embedded with issues of equity, equality and quality that would help in undoing customary practices impacting the status of girls and women.

Women in Maldives have enjoyed a fairly good status in society since its recorded history. There were four ruling queens who ruled this Island nation. They were Sultana Rehendi Kabodi Kilege, Sultana Radafati Kabodi Kilege, Sultana Rehendi Dainu Kabodi Kilege and Hasan Shirazi. These names appear in the early available records and accounts of travellers who visited *Dhivehi Raajje* at different points of time. Some of the available sources also indicate that there were traces of matriarchal society in the past. The social milieu in Maldives past and present

Traditional Maldivian Woman in Dhivehi Raajje

Source: Vilgon, Lars, *Maldive Odd History: The Maldive Archipelago and its People*, Vol.1, Stockholm, 1991.

overtly and covertly was not discriminatory towards girls and women.

The lifecycle of girls from womb to tomb was not marked by any kind of physical or emotional neglect, especially in the areas of food, health, education, care and in their overall growth and development.

Maldive girl smoking water pipe

Source: Vilgon, Lars, *Maldive Odd History: The Maldive Archipelago and its People*, Vol. II, Stockholm, 1992.

Sons and daughters were treated equal by their parents. Reflection of the positive attitude of family and society towards both genders is visible in some of the traditional practices observed in families during childbirth. As soon as a baby is born a ceremony is performed, wherein the family members feed the new born with honey in a spoon with *Sahada* written on it. This initial feeding of the infant marks the initiating ceremony of the baby into the Islamic religion. After seven days of birth, the naming ceremony called *haiduvas* was held. In this ceremony the names of boys and girls are decided. To choose a name, a *Fandita* is called. He chooses names from the Arabic book. Giving of second Arabic name to sons and daughters is a recent practice in Maldives. The practice of a second name began in the Island nation especially when formal schools required it for purposes of identification of children. Father or the *Fandita* then bestows the chosen name by shaving a small piece of hair from the top of the head of the child and a *salavat* is recited. After the ceremony, generally feasting takes place in the family. A special sweet called *bondibai* is prepared and given to the entire family and guests who are present on this auspicious occasion. In fact this practice associated with the birth of a child, continues to exist, even in the contemporary times.

Wife of the Amin, 1899; Maldives family, first family photo, 1883

Source: Vilgon, Lars Maldive *Odd History: The Maldive Archipelago and its People*, Stockholm, 1991-1998.

It is interesting to note that the prevailing socio-economic practices of the past favoured women of this Island nation. There was no dowry system in the Maldives, and this continues till date. Women in Maldives had favourable property rights, a fact that was highlighted in written records. Property was divided according to the *Sharia* with an equal share going to each son, half a share to each daughter and an eighth to the widow. This symbolic aspect which highlights the existence of gender justice in society is also reflected in its traditional system of education.

Traditional education in Dhivehi Raajje was accessible to both the sexes. The Dhivehis were keen to educate their children in religious and temporal subjects. Education of the children was also reflected in the accounts of people who visited the republic from time to time in different capacities. Some of them who mention the educational system were travellers, traders, missionaries and people who visited the Island by default due to shipwreck. Some people who visited this Island wrote about its people and the overall social milieu in an official capacity. The most well known account of government commissioned agent was H.C.P. Bell. In his book on the Maldive Islands: Monograph on the History, Archaeology and Epigraphy, gives in detail the political economic, social, educational and religious practices that were prevalent in Maldives. This book was based on his three visits to Maldives, undertaken during 1879, 1920 and 1922. Along with his work some of the written accounts that give a glimpse of the indigenous system of education are as follows—

Boys and girls studying in traditional school

Source: Dhiraagu Calendar 2007.

> *Education of women in Maldives had a long tradition. Early available records clearly depicts parents' desire to educate their daughters and sons. ..... Maldivians appear to be very well instructed in their language, and most Maldivians, men and women, can read and write it.*
>
> ***Edward Brandis, 1911, p. 205***

Maldivian parents believe in the necessity and importance of intelligent and educated young women.

Edward Dias, 1949, p. 46

Traditional education was domestic in nature. At a tender age of three, boys and girls were instructed by their parents in reciting the holy verses of Quran. Focus was given on memorisation of verses with proper pronunciation. Formal education of children began in private schools or in homes of persons who were influential. The physical structure of traditional schools was very temporary and was largely makeshift in nature. These earlier schools were constructed with locally available materials and had palm thatched roof. In these schools the children studied in the morning. They practised writing on the blackboard covered with white clay. Children were taught to form and pronounce the Arabic letters so that they could "read" the Quran as early as possible. Children were also taught the Dhivehi script. The primary focus of home centred education was on making children correctly memorise the holy Quran. These private schools were begun by older woman or any individual who wanted to do so. In these makeshift arrangements, children would sit engrossed in their lessons, followed by different recreational activities such as playing and other fun loving activities, which were mainly conducted outdoors.

Finances for temporary schools were collectively raised by the community, and the teachers worked voluntarily as part of their traditional obligations. The fee charged from the students was very paltry and could be afforded by most of the parents. As mentioned in the recorded history, the amount charged from parents for education of their ward was two *rufiyaa* a month. It is interesting to note that unlike the traditional education, modern education in Maldives is free for all children, in all Government schools in Male and in the Islands.

The transition of existing indigenous education, to a more formalised structured one, was the beginning of *Maktabs* (primary) and *Madrasas* (higher) centres of learning. The

Maktabs and Madrasas were open to all children. Parents would send their sons and daughters to the *Maktabs*, a practice that bears some kind of similarity with the existing primary educational system prevalent among the Indian Muslims. Higher education in traditional Maldivian society was accessible largely to boys who would enroll themselves in the *Madrasas*. In these *Madrasas* the curriculum mainly consisted of subjects like History, reading, writing Quran and the Arabic script. Education in the *Madrasas* largely depended on the knowledge of the teachers known as *Katibu* or *Kuda Katibu*. Girls were devoid of higher education in the past. In fact Madrasas were mainly accessible to boys.

Reflection of leadership qualities among girls

Source: Kudafaree Madhrasa.

In some Islands there were schools that offered three years of so-called "progressive" education. Teachers appointed in these schools were trained at Male. These trained teachers taught pupils Dhivehi and Arabic languages, Arithmetic and General Knowledge. Some Islands in Maldives also offered five years courses. These courses were available at Naifaru, Huladu and Hitadu Island. Students of these Island schools got certificates from Male. Even though the curriculum was progressive the focus was more on making children have in depth knowledge of the holy Quran so that they imbibe Islamic and human values. As Clarence Maloney in his book *People of the Maldive Islands* mentions—

> *The traditional system of education served to transmit the Great Tradition of Islam and to integrate the Island into the Islamic civilisational system. To that extent it was functional. (p. 237)*

He further added that the traditional system was devoid of encouraging scientific or inquiry based education. He quotes his own experience in this regard—

> *I was asked to give a talk in one of the schools having five grades and three teachers. So I presented the school with a balloon, a globe and talked about it in a very simple manner, translated by a young man who had completed the English High School in Male. The children did not understand the rudimentary ideas I presented about the globe. The teachers did not respond at all, nor say thanks for it (though saying of thanks is not particularly expected). What appears serious to me, however, was the lack of any spark of curiosity about the globe: no student came up to inspect it after the presentation. (p. 236-237)*

Students, who were the recipient of indigenous education, particularly in Male, pursued higher education in Arabic Studies and Urdu. In every generation in the past and in contemporary times, very few students, mainly boys, studied in Cairo, Lucknow and Hyderabad in India and Sri Lanka. After receiving education the students returned to their country to take up higher positions in the government or become teachers to teach Islam and Dhivehi language. This phenomenon continues to exist till date with some changes. Presently students who pursue higher education abroad promote education in different subjects such as sciences, technologies and courses related to tourism and fish processing.

Since Maldives does not have its own university most of the students prefer to pursue higher and professional education outside. The preference of receiving education abroad has now diversified. Students are now keen to opt for European countries and other countries as well that include Australia,

United Kingdom, America, Malaysia and Singapore. Another interesting phenomenon that is visible in the contemporary time is that many women along with their male counterparts also pursue higher and professional education abroad. This fact was elicited from the discussions that were held with some students at the Faculty of Education and Educational Development Centre at Male in 2007*.

While the demand for pursuing higher education is growing in Maldives, the primary education scenario in the Island nation, as mentioned earlier was never a problem. Some of the significant aspects of traditional and the contemporary system of education are marked by the absence of rigidity of customary practices that normally hinder the participation of girls in education, a scenario that is observed in some countries of South Asia including India, such as early marriage and *purdah*. In Maldives veiling was never compulsory for women. Society including parents never forced girls to observe veiling.

A glimpse of morning assembly

Source: Students of Kudafaree Madhrasa.

---

* Based on the study conducted "Srivastava, Gouri, Gender and Peace: Educational Policy Curriculum, English, Environment Studies, Social Studies Textbooks of the Republic of Maldives, 2007, (unpublished report)

In fact veiling of women was not associated with segregation of any kind in the past or the present. Many of the travellers and people who visited this island clearly mentioned that women of Maldives were never forced to veil. Given below are excerpts from some of the written sources—

Reflection of tradition and modernity in the dresses worn by Maldivian women

Source: Staff and Students of Muhyiddin School, Villingili Island.

> *Although it is a Moslem country women do not go veiled....*
>
> This fact is also corroborated in the account of H.C.P Bell he states—
>
> *All the inhabitants of these Islands are subject to a chief, who convokes them, and protects and defends them to the best of his power.*
> *His wife administers justice, and speaks in public unveiled, after an established custom from which they never vary.* (p. 17)

Another interesting phenomenon that reflects the absence of rigidity among the Maldivians is regarding the dress of their children. In the past parents would dress their boys and girls in similar manner. During infancy and early childhood girls and boys wore the same dress that comprised a waist cloth only and the upper portion of the body remained bare. However, girls were dressed differently after puberty. The attire of women is also mentioned in detail in some of the written sources.

Maldive girl pounding rice and traditional Maldive women making lace and smoking water pipe

Source: Vilgon, Lars, *Maldive Odd History: The Maldive Archipelago and its People*, Vol. I, Stockholm, 1991.

The traditional Maldivian women invariably wear a waist cloth, chocolate in colour, relieved by black and white stripes, called a *feyli.* A smock or chemise like upper garment reaches to the knees, chiefly of dark blue or terracotta, with sleeves tight fitting at the wrist and with a yoke at the neck cut fairly low, and edged with red or blue or yellow embroidery. A coloured handkerchief rolled round the coil of the thick dark hair made up into a knot on the right side of the head completes the attire.

Some of the women wore bangles on the wrist and the better classes also wore necklaces, earrings and other kinds of jewellery. Girls were dressed in the same way as boys until they reached nine or ten years, only wearing the waist cloth and leaving the upper portion of the body bare. However, in contemporary times the dresses of both men and women have changed. The traditional dress is very rarely worn by women now-a-days. They wear it only on special occasions.

The egalitarian nature of Maldivians finds a mention in the Census of 1911. The Census states that the female children appeared to be treated with same care as the males. This was also true in the context of health, food and overall care, as mentioned earlier. Regarding the age of marriage, Pyrard, a French traveller, writes—

Source: Vilgon, Lars, *Maldive Odd History: The Maldive Archipelago and its People*, Vol. V, Stockholm, 1995.

The males may marry when they will, but a female orphan cannot marry till she is fifteen. If the girl's father is alive, he would at times marry his daughter at the age of 10 or 11 to the first suitor whether old or young, provided his quality is in some measure suitable to hers... Most of the Maldivian reckon it a sin to keep theirs daughters unmarried, a practice that bears a close resemblance to those existing among the Hindus.

The institution of marriage in Maldives did not debar girls from receiving education. None of the accounts of travellers or earlier work on Maldives mentions this practice. Thus, the traditional system of education contributed in helping 80% Dhivehis to read and write. According to 1911 census the literacy rate of the Republic was very impressive. In every inhabited Island education was available to all children, even though it was rudimentary in form.

Girl on swing

Source: Vilgon, Lars, *Maldive Odd History: The Maldive Archipelago and its People*, Vol. 1, Stockholm, 1991.

Scene of joyful learning

Source: Students of Galholhu Madhrasa, Male.

Table 4.1 : Percentage of Literates, 1911, by Sex and Age Groups

Name of Atoll	*Literates*							
	Males				*Females*			
	0-10	*10-15*	*15-20*	*20 and over*	*0-10*	*10-15*	*15-20*	*20 and over*
Maldive Islands	3	41	60	72	4	45	60	71
Male Atoll	6	40	64	71	7	47	66	69
Nilandi Atoll	3	40	65	74	5	46	67	69
Mulaka Atoll	12	57	66	81	9	69	80	80
Fadiffolu Atoll	8	46	64	70	8	52	66	65
Felidi Atoll	12	51	76	88	13	62	78	88
Kolumadulu Atoll	5	46	65	78	9	52	81	75
Ari Atoll	8	39	61	69	5	41	54	58
Miladumma-dulu Atoll	0.4	22	48	63	1	27	44	54
Malosmadulu Atoll	0.4	27	46	64	0.4	27	49	60
Hadummati Atoll	1	19	38	56	2	24	41	59
Addo Atoll	1	84	91	90	1	85	91	95
Tiladumati Atoll	0.4	19	39	54	0.2	15	32	39
Male Island	8	62	82	94	14	71	83	89
Huwadu Atoll	2	54	68	82	4	55	68	81

Source: H.C.P. Bell, *The Maldives Islands, Monograph on the History, Archaeology and Epigraphy*, p. 203.

From the above table it appears that in the inhabited Islands of Maldives, the gap in the literacy rate among men and women in different age groups was minimal. In some Islands the literacy of women was higher than men, e.g. in Addo Atoll, Male Island and in Felidi Atoll.

It is interesting to note that girls in Maldives loved to play outdoor games. One such popular sport was *Bashi*. This game is popular among girls and adult women even to this day.

Girls playing the traditional *Bashi* game

Source: Gaafu Alifu Atoll.

Thus, among the South Asian Countries, Maldives and Sri Lanka are perhaps the only countries having a legacy of favourable educational indicators for both the sexes. In contemporary times both these countries enjoy high literacy and enrolment rate for both sexes. This positive scenario along with an unbiased system of education helped women to seek opportunities in the arena of available employment.

The main profession that women were engaged in the past was mainly confined to household activities. Besides this women were involved in traditional crafts, such as lace making, coir ropes and in all activities that related to fish processing, such as cleaning, boiling, smoking and drying. These activities needed no formal guidance. Women engaged in such activities learned it by observing senior women of the household. This phenomena can be compared to the Indian situation. In the nineteenth century formal institution of educations were devoid of women scholars. This was due to the fact that education of women was not seen as essential. Household chores, it was felt, could be learnt through practice and observation of senior women in the family.

A few women in Maldives also took to teaching as a profession in the capital city of Male. An interesting account of the professional status of women is mentioned in the 1911 Census. This document portrays that 56% of the female population of Maldives earned their own living.

Lace Making : Collars and Cuffs of Women's Libaas

Source: Dhiraagu Calender, 2007.

> Among the arts and crafts of Maldives lace making was important. It was mainly done by women. The lace was often made with gold and silver thread imported from India and was to ornament the upper portion of the dress worn by the Maldivian women. Weaving exquisite handloom cloth with silk and coloured with indigenous vegetable dyes was another important contribution of women of Dhivehi Raajje.

Pounding the fibers out of the husk for preparing coir ropes

Source: Dhiraagu Calender, 2007.

Gender Minister Aishath Mohamed Didi with the author and Woman making a coir rope on Kulhudufushi

Source: Male, 2007 and Neville, Adrian, Dhivehi Raajje: 1993-95, A Portrait of Maldives, Seven Holidays.

Beginning of Modern Education: Women's Education

Systematic formal education in Maldives began in 1927 with the introduction of secondary level schooling in Male by the then Prime Minister Amir Abdul Majeed. He established Madhrsathul Sanniyya which later branched out into two important schools for boys and girls. Majeediyya was for boys and Aminiyya for girls. In 1948, in each of the four wards of Male, two schools were established, one for girls and other for boys. In these schools, besides the teaching of lslam and Quran, subjects such as Arithmetic, History, Geography and Dhivehi were taught. English, Arabic and Urdu were taught as second languages.

Indian and Maldivian teachers of Villingili School

Source: Villingili, 2007.

In connection with girls' education, a pioneering initiative was undertaken by Mr. Amin Didi, the first President of Maldives. He commissioned a batch of 14 girls to be sent to Sri Lanka in 1940 and 1950 to pursue higher education. Girls, who were sent to Sri Lanka, were accommodated in a large bungalow in a place called Bambalapitiya under the direct supervision of a House Mistress and the Representative of the Maldivian Government in Sri Lanka. Maldivian girls in Sri Lanka received their formal education in a school run by missionaries called the Holy Family Convent. One of the students of this school, Habeeba Hussain Habeeba, became the first teacher of a formal school called Saniyya, in Male. She was the Executive Director at the National Library Male in 2007. Besides acquiring formal education, in Sri Lanka girls learned music and housecraft in their hostel.

Source: Vilgon, Lars, Maldives Odd History: The Maldive Archipelago and its People, Stockholm, 1991-1998.

The enrolment of Maldivian girls in convent schools was an innovative and pioneering initiative of parents. It shows that Maldivian society was not rigid. Although 100% Dhivehis are Sunni Muslims they had no reservation about their daughters being taught in convents. This phenomenon also reflects the flexibility and adaptability of the Maldivian society in the past.

The year 1960 was important in the educational history of Maldives. It saw the merger of traditional system of education with the Western system of education. The commingling of indigent and alien systems of education resulted in English becoming the medium of education. This medium replaced Dhivehi language which was the spoken language of the people. There were several reasons for this gradual transition of medium. Among several reasons cited, the most important was the growing phenomena of globalisation, liberalisation and consumerisation. The Maldivian economy from the late nineteenth century onwards began to be linked with the world economy in a substantial manner. Imports and exports with different countries of the world necessitated the adoption of English as a link language of communication. Speaking, listening and writing of English language became crucial for all Maldivians seeking employment in all the sectors of the economy. As a result, schools in Maldives began to change over to English as a subject and as a medium of education. This change in the medium of education in the Republic of Maldives was much later when compared to India. In India, English became the official medium of instruction as early as 1835. In Maldives the Majeediya and Aminiyya schools for boys and girls were the first to switch over to English as the medium of education. These schools gradually introduced University of London Secondary School Curriculum and held the first G.C.E. Ordinary Level Examination in 1967. They also prepared students for the London Chambers of Commerce. Further, the need to promote science education in the country led to the establishment of Science Educational Centre in 1979. This Centre prepared students to sit for the London G.C.E. Advanced Level Examination which qualified them for University Education overseas.

In 1980, the Government of Maldives wanted to spread education in different Islands and bring the education system of the country under a unified system of education. In each Atoll of the country, primary schools and Atoll Educational Centre, were established. With the establishment of these Educational Centres, opportunities for education of boys and girls increased manifold. However, as compared to girls more boys completed higher levels of education. One of the reasons for lower access of girls to higher education was the absence of residential schools in distantly located Islands, and parents lacking confidence to send their daughters to other Islands including Male for higher professional education. It was observed during 2007 that many schools in the Islands still do not have residential facilities for girls. In a discussion held with some parents staying in different Islands of the Republic in 2007, it was found that they were not very comfortable with educating their daughters outside the Island. They were concerned about the safety of their daughters. The growing instances of child abuse and drug consumption among children made the parents insecure and reluctant to send their children to stay with their relatives or friends either in Male or Islands having facilities for higher education.

However, this scenario is gradually undergoing a change. With the expansion of information technology and the growing demand of skilled human power there is a conscious effort on the part of the government to enhance and upgrade the quality of physical and other infrastructure facilities. Besides this, efforts are being made to eradicate the menace of child abuse and drug peddling by the Gender Ministry. It is hoped that these changes would motivate parents to send their children to schools, especially girls. Schools in most of the Islands are being upgraded and provision of new technologies, e.g. computers with internet facilities, are being provided. Some of the primary schools in the Islands have secondary schooling facilities. In Naifaru boarding facilities for children are being made. This was observed in 2007.

In the changing socio-economic scenario of this Island nation and with the growth and expansion of tourism and other service sectors, the demand for skilled and trained human capital is growing day by day. This trend has compelled the government in the Republic to lay greater stress on vocational and technical education.

Contemporary changes in Maldives have also affected women and their contributions to the traditional economy of Maldives. As mentioned earlier, prior to tourism, women in Maldives contributed to fishing and its processing in a substantial manner. Some of the activities that were women centric were drying, smoking, slating and processing of fish, till about 1970s. However, with the introduction of mechanisation in fish processing, women have now lost their traditional role in this important economic activity. With the introduction of new technologies in freezing and mechanisation, it is now possible to sell fishes directly to collector vessels. Thus, the introduction of modern technology in this particular sector has had a twin and contradictory impact. On the one hand it has helped in enhancing production of processed fish and on the other hand it has eroded women's role in fish processing.

Drying and smoking of fish

Source: Neville, Adrian, *Dhivehi Raajje: 1993-95, A Portrait of Maldives, Seven Holidays.*

The positive scenario witnessed in the introduction of modern technology in fishing has led to upscaling the demand of skilled human power. Training of boys and girls in innovative ways of fish processing has created a need for skill based education. Many Maldivian students seek this skill in fishing and various other vocations in different countries of the world. While a few go abroad, some also pursue higher education in their own country for getting better paid jobs. Scholarships are increasingly sought by students. Table 4.2 gives an account of scholarships received by students according to gender.

Table 4.2 : Students who Received Scholarships during 2005

Year	Total	Diploma		Degree		Masters		Ph.D.	
		Male	Female	Male	Female	Male	Female	Male	Female
2005	139	9	4	60	53	5	5	0	3

Source: Department of Higher Education and Training.

Table 4.2 depicts an interesting trend. In context of diploma, the number of males who were recipients of scholarship was more as compared to the females. Degree course also depicted the same trend. Master course had equal number of male and female students who received the scholarships. For pursuing Ph.D. in different disciplines, scholarships were availed only by women.

In contemporary times some important educational changes initiated by the government have stabilised the retention rates of Maldivian children in different schools. Motivational schemes like making education free to all, provision of textbooks, and taking steps for addressing the needs of children with disability, are some significant steps geared to achieve the EFA and Millennium Development goals. Government had also formulated a Draft National Policy on Disability in 2007. Government policy and the existing social milieu in the Republic have had a positive impact. Students who are keen to pursue higher education are given requisite facilities and scholarships. Table 4.3 gives a graphic picture about courses and the educational scenario in the Republic in 2005.

Table 4.3 : Students Enrolment in Maldives College of Higher Education by Faculties and Sex, 2005

Faculties	*Both Sexes*	*Male (%)*	*Female (%)*
Foundation Studies (FS)	440	134 **(30.5)**	306 **(69.5)**
Centre for Open Learning (COL)	389	67 **(17.2)**	322 **(82.8)**
Centre for Maritime Studies (CMS)	13	13 **(100)**	0
Faculty of Education (FE)	764	210 **(27.5)**	554 **(72.5)**
Faculty of Engineering and Technology	234	227 **(97)**	7 **(3)**
Faculty of Health Science (FHS)	170	9 **(5.3)**	161 **(94.7)**
Faculty of Management and Computing (FMC)	324	173 **(53.4)**	151 **(46.6)**
Faculty of Shariah and Law (FSL)	41	17 **(41.5)**	24 **(58.5)**
Total	2375	850	1525

Source: Statistical Yearbook of Maldives, 2006, p. 93 (Figures in the bracket are percentages).

From Table 4.3, it appears that most of the female students enrolled themselves at the Faculty of Education, followed by Centre of Open Learning and Foundation Studies. The enrolment of males is greater at the Faculty of Engineering and Technology followed by Faculty of Education and Faculty of Management and Computing. This table also shows that there is a bit of stereotyping in choice of courses opted by the girls. In Maldives teaching is a popular profession among women in Male and in the Islands. It is one of the largest service sectors of the economy that employs women. In a discussion held with the teachers of different schools in Male in 2007, they were of the opinion that the main reason for making teaching a popular profession among women is that it is the only profession that helps them to balance household chores with demands of profession commitments. It is also culturally and socially acceptable by the community. Given below is Table 4.4 that depicts employment of population in different sectors.

Girls being trained for defence

Source: Aminiya School, Male.

Table 4.4 : Employed Population by Industry, Occupation and Sex, 2000

Occupation	*Males*	*Females*	*Total*
Legislators, Senior Officials and Managers	3,228	587	3,815
Professionals	3,917	3,687	7,604
Technicians and Associate Professionals	4,432	1,931	6,363
Clerks	2,399	2,212	4,611
Service workers, and shop and market sales workers	8,486	2,068	10,554
Skilled Agricultural and Fisheries Workers	10,133	1,432	11,565
Craft and related Trade Workers	8,680	5,838	14,518
Plant, Machine Operators, Assemblers	4,954	125	5,079
Elementary Occupations	4,327	1,831	6,158
Armed Forces	1,351	82	1,433
Not Stated	5,444	9,101	14,545

Source: Statistical Yearbook of Maldives, 2006, p. 62.

From the above table it is seen that professions popular among women in Maldives in the present times are craft and related trade works. Professions that are popular with men are related to all service sectors of the economy. Men are employed as service workers, sales persons in markets, as technicians and as Associate Professors. Besides crafts, women are also employed in the education sector in different capacities as academicians and in the administration. The government and private sectors also employ women in the lower runks as clerks and computer operators. Sectors that have very few women employed are Armed Forces and industry specialising in plant and machine operations.

Thus, women's education in the past and present depicts that the *Dhivehi Rajje* had a rich legacy of women's education. Religion and culture were never barriers for acquisition of knowledge by the children of the Republic. However, higher education was very limited in the context of girls in the earlier days and continues so even to this day. In the present times as mentioned earlier, the Republic does not have a university for higher education. Very few women, including women from affluent backgrounds, pursue higher education outside their country. Discussions held with some students who were from ordinary backgrounds at the Faculty of Education revealed that at times funding and getting scholarships from the government and foreign agencies was problematic.

Niuma Ahmed is the second Island chief of Baa Atoll, Eydhafushi Island. She is also the vice president of the women committee of the Island.
Issues currently taken up by her—*Problems related to divorce, domestic violence, child abuse cases, empowering housewives, visit school on behalf of parents who are unable to participate and ensuring that committed teachers are appointed in the Island schools.*

Women in Governance

Thus, while higher education is yet to get universalised, the Republic has succeeded in universalising education at the primary level. Apparently Maldives is close to the EFA goals; however, the quality of education is yet to be addressed. In fact, the present system of education has not been able to address some of the conflicting situations affecting society in a big way, i.e. growing divorce rate, child abuse and drug trafficking. These prevailing social problems impact family ties and adversely affect children of all age groups. In a discussion held with stakeholders in 2007, it emerged that the intensity of the above-mentioned problems was more in Male as compared to other Islands. One of the reasons cited was overpopulation and overcrowding of living spaces. This negative aspect of urbanisation impacted the emotional and physical growth of children. Perhaps this could have led to the growth of child abuse, intake of drugs adversely impacting the status of women in the Maldivian society.

Therefore, even though the social milieu and cultural practices support education of girls, certain prevalent social practices adversely impact the status of women. They include the growing incidence of physical and emotional violence against women and girls. A Study on Women's Health and Life Experiences conducted by the Ministry of Gender and Family with technical assistance from the World Health Organisation and financial support from UNFPA and UNICEF in 2006 highlighted the extent of physical and emotional violence that women and girls encounter on a daily basis. Some of the reported facts stated in the study are as follows—

- In the Maldives, 1 in 5 women aged 15-49, who have ever been in a relationship, reported experiencing some form of physical or sexual violence by an intimate partner.
- 6.3% of women aged 15-49, who have ever been pregnant, reported being physically or sexually abused during pregnancy. Of those abused during pregnancy 41% reported being punched or kicked in the abdomen.
- Women who have experienced intimate partner violence are significantly more likely to report miscarriage, stillbirths and abortions.
- 1 in 9 women aged 15-49 reported experiencing severe physical violence by an intimate partner such as being punched, kicked, chocked or burnt or having a weapon used against them.
- Women who have experienced physical or sexual partner violence are twice as likely to report poor or very poor general health compared with women who have not experienced partner violence.
- 1 in 6 women in Male aged 15-49 reported having experienced childhood sexual abuse (under the age of 15). The rate is 1 in 8 for the whole country.
- 30% of women aged 15-49, who have ever been in a relationship, reported experiencing emotional abuse by an intimate partner.
- The level of emotional distress of women who have experienced physical or sexual partner violence is more than twice as high as for those not experiencing partner violence.
- All together 1 in 3 Maldivian women aged 15-49 reported experiencing some form of physical or sexual violence at least once during their lifetime.

Thus, the positive educational scenario that has ensured access to all children up to primary level, coupled with high literacy rate among men and women has not ensured quality education. This phenomena depicts that literacy and status of women are very often not positively correlated. Education policy and other motivational programmes of the government have attempted to address only the practical needs of the children of Maldives. The strategic needs that encompass transformative systematic change in the society and in the existing gender relations remain to be addressed.

Thus, women in the contemporary Maldivian Society like their South Asian counterparts face a dilemma between their ascribed and achieved status. Globalisation, consumerism, growing regional identity and to a limited extent, fundamentalism have visibly and invisibly created a paradoxical situation between equity and equality. Thus overtly and covertly the status of Maldivian women in contemporary timing can best be described as a mix between tradition and modernity.

REFERENCES

Bell, H.C.P., Op. cit.

Cambridge Education: Strengthening the Framework of Education Towards Vision 2020, Draft Final Report, Prepared by Cambridge Education, 18 December, 2005.

Denham, Edward Brandis, Census of 1911, the Maldives.

Dias, Edward, Op. cit.

Hockly, T.W., 1940. *A Short Account of the People, History and Customs of the Maldives Archipelago*, H.F. and G. Witherby, London.

Maloney, C., 1980, *People of the Maldives Island*, Orient Longman, New Delhi.

Srivastava, Gouri. 2007. Gender and Peace: Educational Policy Curriculum, English, Environment Studies, Social Studies textbooks of the Republic of Maldives, (unpublished report).

Srivastava, Gouri. 2000. Women's Higher Education in the 19th Century, Concept Publishing Company Pvt. Ltd., New Delhi.

Statistical Year Book of Maldives 2006, Ministry of Planning and National Development Male, Maldives.

5

Some Challenges and Road Maps that Need Addressing

Policies and programmes need to address both practical gender needs and initiate transformatory changes for ushering human face of development.

The Millennium Development Goals (MDGs)—

- Eradicate extreme poverty and hunger
- Achieve universal primary education
- Promote gender equality and empower women
- Reduce child mortality
- Improve maternal health
- Combat HIV/AIDS, malaria and other diseases
- Ensure environmental sustainability
- Develop a global partnership for development.

The new millennium has set an important agenda globally that has become guiding philosophy for all nations of the world. A major declaration signed by one hundred forty seven countries of the world popularly known as the 'Millennium Development Goals' (MDGs) has set road maps for countries striving to achieve human face of development with inclusion of gender justice, harmony and peace.

It is hoped that working towards MDGs would in the long run help member countries address social conflicts such as racism, ethnicity, religion, gender based violence, drug trafficking, cross border disputes and those related to human-made and natural disasters impacting human survival.

Member countries the world over have adopted a plethora of strategies for achieving these well laid out goals by 2015. The Republic of Maldives is also on the move. Like many other nations of the world it is meticulously designing strategies to meet the set targets in a stipulated time span. In the present chapter an attempt has been made to discuss in detail two of the MDGs, i.e. achievement of Universal Primary Education (UPE) and promotion of Gender Equality (GE). The focus would be to see whether these two goals can be met by the Republic by 2015.

As stated in the earlier chapters in terms of quantitative educational indicators, the educational scenario in Maldives apparently seems very favourable. In fact, along with Sri Lanka, this Republic in South Asia, can proudly claim of having an overall good educational scenario. While it is very heartening to see that all children go to school in the Republic, a major area of concern during field visits and discussions, that were held with all stakeholders in 2007, was related to quality issue in education. The challenges that the Republic faces in contemporary time is addressing the paradoxical situation, i.e. gap between quantity and quality indicators in education. Given below are some of the challenges that were observed during fieldwork.

- Availability of teachers and their capacity building
- English as a medium of education
- Expansion of vocational and technical education
- Child abuse and divorces
- Drug peddling
- Environment degradation and the rising sea levels

The above-mentioned challenges have highlighted the systemic crisis that the Republic is encountering. Even though attempts have been made for addressing these hurdles, a lot more focused efforts are needed for achieving the MDGs.

Availability of Teachers and their Capacity Building

In the Republic of Maldives the educational sector has made considerable progress, as stated in chapters 2, 3 and 4. Further this aspect was visible in terms of quantitative expansion of schools, availability of incentives such as free education to all children and textbooks. Existing physical facilities in all government schools were satisfactory and the maintenance was relatively good. Added to this phenomena was the availability of teachers in different disciplines such as Science, Social Science, Maths, English, Dhivehi and Physical Education at the Elementary stage. The existing scenario of students and teachers in Educational Institutions by Locality in 2005 is mentioned in Table 5.1.

Table 5.1 : Students and Teachers in Educational Institutions by Locality, 2005

Locality	*No. of*	*Students*	*Teachers*			*Student*
	Schools	*Enrol-ment*	*Trained*	*Untrained*	*Total*	*teacher ratio (Trained teachers)*
Male	22	30,036	1,015	286	1,301	29.59
Atoll	312	72,037	2,317	1,998	4,315	31.09
Republic	334	102,073	3,332	2,284	5,616	30.63

Source: School Statistics-2005, Ministry of Education.

From the above table it appears that the total number of trained teachers in Male and Atoll was more than untrained teachers.

Despite the number of trained teachers being more than untrained, the Republic faced problems of quality teaching and learning in subjects like Science, Maths and English. This was observed during classroom observations in all schools in Male and in the few Islands. In all the twenty-four schools that were visited, it was observed that physical expansion of schools in the Republic had not kept pace with the demand and availability of trained and qualified teachers. In most of the cases local teachers possessed, G.C.E. 'O' Level and 'A' Level certification, with few teachers having primary, middle and secondary certification in school teaching. For compensating the shortage of well qualified and trained teachers the Republic employed and continues to employ a substantial number of expatriate teachers. The recruited teachers were mainly from India, Sri Lanka, Pakistan and Bangladesh. Very few were from European countries. At the time of focus group discussions in 2007, some of the teachers reported that they had teaching experience in their respective countries, but did not have a formal certification from a Teacher Training Institute. This was mainly true of teachers who were from Pakistan and Bangladesh.

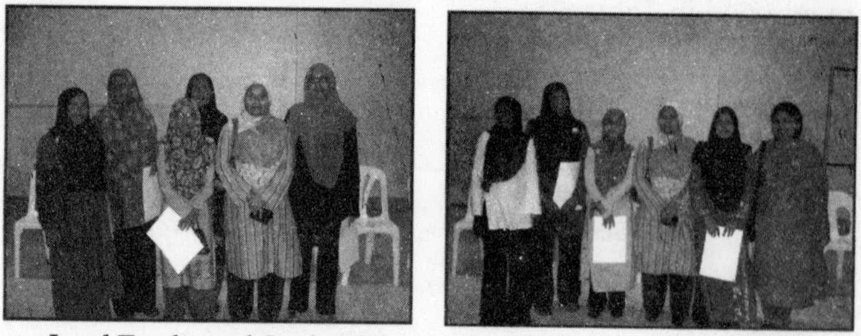

Local Teachers of Gaafu Alifu Island and Resource Persons from Education Development Centre

Source: Gaafu Alifu Island, 2007.

Table 5.2 depicts the status of professional training of Teachers in schools that were visited in Male and Islands.

Table 5.2 : Professional Status of Teachers in the Republic

	Male			*Female*		
	Trained	*Untrained*	*Total*	*Trained*	*Untrained*	*Total*
Expatriate	17	10	28	20	13	33
Local	5	8	12	15	7	22
Total	22	18	40	35	20	55

Source: Data derived from questionnaire administered to teachers in 2007 in Male and in few visited Islands.

As stated earlier, most of the teachers employed in Maldives were of Indian origin. They belong to the states of Kerala, Karnataka and Tamil Nadu. A few were from Sri Lanka, Pakistan and Bangladesh. Most of the expatriate teachers of

Indian origin were professionally trained. They had M.Ed. and B.Ed. degrees in Education. Trained local teachers possessed the following qualifications—Certification in Primary, Middle and Secondary School teaching.

The lack of sufficient trained local teachers had necessitated the employment of large number of expatriate teachers at the lower secondary schools. In 2005, about 1% of the teachers employed in the pre-primary, 16% of the teachers employed in the primary, 72% of the teachers in the lower secondary and 77% in the higher secondary were expatriates.

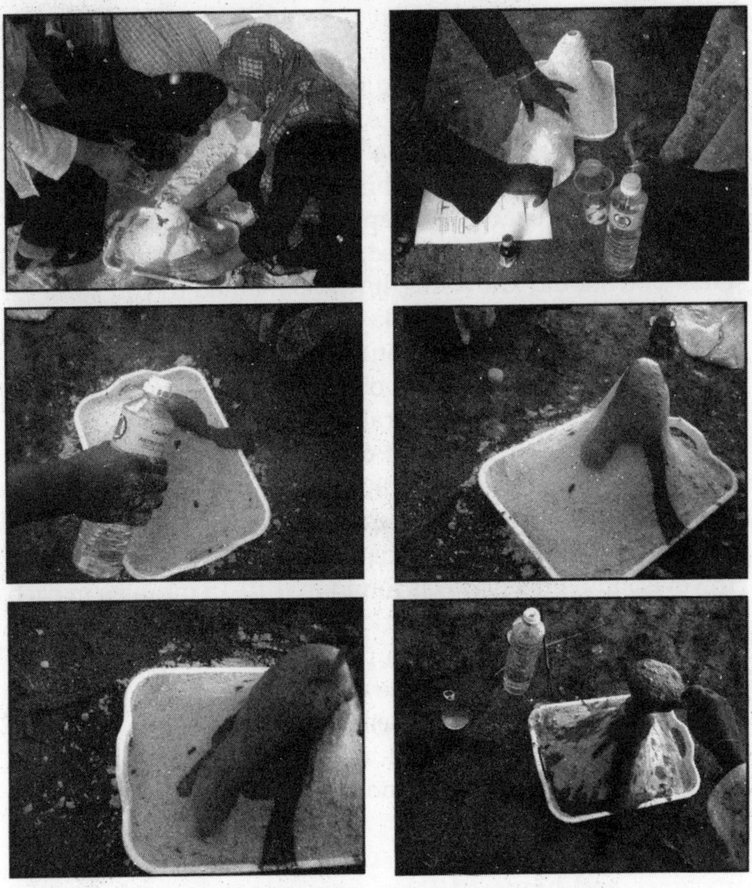

Teachers preparing a module on volcanic eruption

Source: Gaafu Alifu Atoll, 2007.

In classroom observations, especially in the domain of Environmental Studies, Social Science and English, it was found that all the teachers had prepared lesson plans. These plans were meticulously carried by them and were placed in the classroom at a convenient place. Initial teaching in Male and Island schools was teacher centred. Around ten to fifteen minutes of classroom teaching was focused on lecture method, followed by the adoption of different participatory techniques. They were—quiz, riddles and the use of different types of innovative games. However, during participatory sessions in all classroom observations very few children were communicative and expressive. Some of the students who participated were not very confident in speaking English. In some schools such as Madhrasathul Aliya, Maafannu Madhrasa and Madhrasathul Ahmadhiya children were very confident in expressing themselves in their mother tongue, i.e. *Dhivehi.* In 50% cases the lessons that were observed in social science and languages were repeated. Before the beginning of any lessons that were observed, the teachers would normally state "You should know this, it was explained to you earlier, I have done it with you yesterday, please try and recall."

In connection with content delivery of the above-mentioned disciplines it was observed that even though the teachers of expatriate and local origins were knowledgeable and were aware of the latest developments in their subject areas, the approach adopted in teaching and evaluation was traditional. In most of the cases it was textbook oriented and teacher centred. This approach varied between schools. However, universally it was found that 10-15 minutes in each class was devoted to pedagogical processes that was teacher oriented. During focus group discussions held with the teachers, they reported that they were compelled to adopt this pedagogical technique, as students were not able to understand concepts related to the above-mentioned subjects. They also stated that schools in Male and in the Islands lacked crucial facilities such as reference materials in Social Science, Science, Maths, and English. This impacted the teaching and learning processes and hindered them from adopting participatory approaches.

It was strongly suggested by teachers as well as parents that the schools in the Republic needed well equipped libraries with textbooks and supplementary materials related to the disciplines of Social Studies, Sciences, Maths and English for addressing needs of learners and to enable them to understand difficult concepts. They suggested that procurement of textual materials prepared by different publishers should be made on a priority basis. Science teachers were of the view that absence of science labs in a few Male and Island schools impacted the development of experimental methods in science teaching. Thus, application of textual knowledge in sciences and environmental studies to understand natural phenomena could not be practically done by teachers. In connection with content updation, one common issue that emerged in classroom observation and discussions held with the teachers was the lack of in-service training in subject specific areas and in the methodology of teaching. This included training in Information and Communication Technology (ICT). The teachers reported that the training they received was mainly done by the

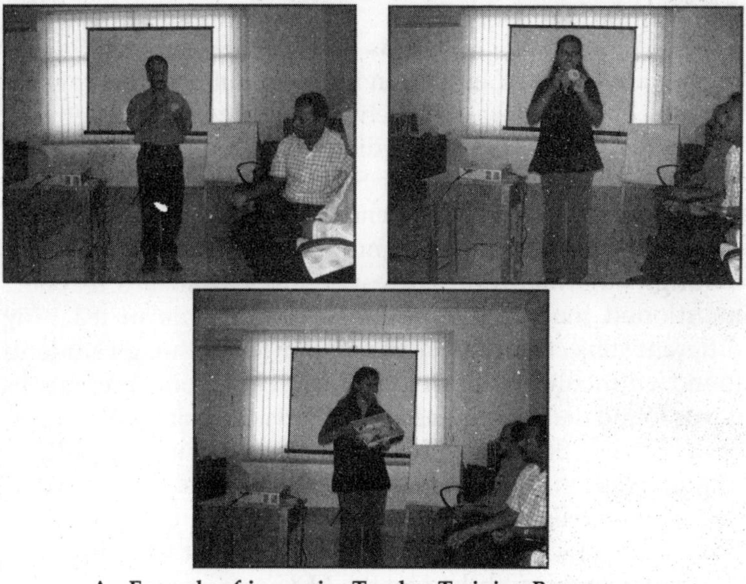

An Example of in-service Teacher Training Programme

Source: Gaafu Alifu Atoll, 2007.

Educational Development Centre (EDC). However, the training given was not sufficient. There was consensus among the teachers that in-service training should be given more frequently (at least two to three times in a year) preferably, before the beginning and after the academic sessions.

Besides these, the expatriate teachers mentioned certain common concerns that need short term and long term addressing.

- Salaries of the teachers need to be revised in accordance with the cost of living index
- Setting up of committee to address problems of expatriate teachers
- Ensuring safety and security of expatriate women teachers
- Organisation of programmes for training expatriate teachers in *Dhivehi* language and Maldivian culture.

Medium of Education

The medium of education was another factor responsible for impacting quality of education in the Republic. Teaching and learning of English was a perceived challenge that the Republic faced. The switching of the medium of education from Dhivehi to English at Primary, Lower Secondary and the Secondary levels did not promote confidence in the students in speaking, reading, listening and in communicating different subjects through this medium. However, the expatriate teachers mentioned that they were more comfortable in teaching different subjects through this medium, even though students found it difficult. During fieldwork and classroom observations it was found that all subjects, particularly Environment Studies, Social Studies, Sciences and Maths, were taught in this medium. English was taught as a core subject at all levels. All prescribed textual materials were available to children in English. At the primary level textual materials in English that were in use in all schools were published by the EDC.

During classroom observations and discussions held with teachers in Male schools and in the Islands, they mentioned that children used both languages, i.e. Dhivehi and English. In the context of English, speaking as well as writing was a major challenge. In many cases, in the pronunciation as well as in the construction of sentences, the grammar used by children was often incorrect. Very few students were confident in English. In primary grades girls were not very communicative in English. In lower secondary grades, 40% students were not very fluent in English language. Very often local teachers and very few expatriate teachers used *Dhivehi* language for clearing the concepts of pupils. Translation of terms in Science and Social Science was frequently done in *Dhivehi* by the teachers. In one of the Island schools located at Noonu Atoll, the Social Studies teacher was teaching the subject in *Dhivehi* and occasionally using English for clearing concepts and difficult words in the subject. During discussions that were organised with the teachers belonging to different disciplines, it was reported that the children in the Republic, understood the subject better in their mother tongue. In Male the Almadharasathul Arabiyathul Islamiyya School adopted a three language formula. Subjects like Social Studies, Environmental Studies were imparted to the students in English, *Dhivehi* and in the Arabic mediums. The principal mentioned that the performance of children was good in all the three mediums. He further elaborated that children were free to choose any medium of instruction based on their comprehension and fluency in the language.

In curriculum plus activities that included dramatics, music, indoor and outdoor sports, children generally spoke in *Dhivehi* language. In connection with difficulties encountered in English language, some of the teachers were of the view that it related to the home environment. The skills of speaking, listening and communicating in English could not be practised at home as parents and peers hardly used this language in their day-to-day interactions. In fact, the use of English remained confined to the teaching and learning processes in the classrooms.

It is interesting to note that while the children found difficulty in expressing themselves in English, they were very keen to learn it. Some of the reasons cited by them are mentioned below.

School children participating in school band and girls participating in march past

Source: Jamaluddin School, Male, 2007 and Aminiya School, Male, 2007.

Reasons for learning English as a First and Second Language

- Knowing English language was the need of the hour as it helped them understand concepts in Sciences and Maths.
- It is a global language and it helped them in getting connected with children from different countries and would help them have a better understanding about places, cultures, traditions, and lives and conditions of the people.
- Most of the audio-video media adopt this language.
- Knowing English would help them pursue their interests in English music, serials and cartoons shows.
- The language has immense economic value as it would enable them to get employment in tourist resorts and other service sectors.

Creativity of children being appreciated by the principal and teachers

Source: Kudafaree Madhrasa, 2007.

For improving their skills in English language, students adopted multiple strategies. Some of them got their doubts cleared from their peers and teachers, and some attended tuition classes. In the discussions held with students a few of them were of the view that schools should arrange extra classes for all children in English. Two students in one of the Island schools, i.e. Kudafaree Madhrasa, were of the view that the holy Quran should be translated into English.

Expansion of Vocational and Technical Education

A crucial emerging issue impacting the overall educational scenario in the Republic was the need of promoting vocational and technical education at the secondary level. The high cost of living index, coupled with poverty of households compelled parents to force their sons and daughters to earn their living while they were studying. This affected their academic performance. In Maafannu Madharus the principal and teachers mentioned that children who were not performing well in academics were those who were involved in domestic work or in different income generating activities.

Efforts to address this issue had already being taken by the government. There was a move to diversify secondary education by including vocational subjects. Training was gradually being introduced in the secondary schools and trained technical trainees were provided. Further, the Ministry of Education had launched vocational subjects in Male, and then gradually expanded these courses to selected secondary schools in the Atolls. For promoting vocational education the government had established Vocational Educational Centres in three Focus Islands, as part of the Tsunami recovery and reconstruction effort.

Though, steps taken by the government in this regard were commendable, they were not enough or substantial to address the diverse needs and choices of the students at the secondary stages. Many of the boys and a few girls at the secondary stages, especially in the Islands, were not aware of vocational and technical courses in different countries including their own Islands. Further they were not sure about the courses they would opt for in future.

Phenomena of Child Abuse and Divorce

One of the major issues impacting quality education was the prevalence of child abuse and divorce. This problem has already been stated in earlier chapters. This social malaise particularly affected adolescent children physically and emotionally. During fieldwork undertaken in Male schools and in the Islands, and discussions held with all the stakeholders, it was reported that child abuse was more Male centric, than an Island issue. Among several reasons that were cited by all stakeholders, the most important one was related to the growing urbanisation of Male. As compared to different Islands of the Republic, Male offered and continues to offer till date, greater educational and employment opportunities. Many government offices and business establishments are located in Male. Thus, greater job opportunities are available to all job seekers.

The existing employment opportunities facilitated influx of people from Islands to this capital city. Another reason quoted by the people was that migration to Male had also increased manifold after the occurrence of Tsunami. Continuous migration of people had led to overcrowding of living spaces. Most of the houses (mainly flats) had two to three families residing together. Large families living in limited spaces had thrown up major social problems such as child abuse. Parents reported that very often the perpetrator of this crime was a close family member. Teachers and the Principal were of the opinion that many of the conflicting situations and tension in the schools were due to children who were victims of this ghastly practice. A victimised child often became a problematic case for the school. This was visible in the peculiar behavioural traits of the child. The use of abusive language, adoption of defiant attitude and violent behaviour with peers and teachers led to disruption of school environment.

The mechanism for tackling children with behavioural problems had been very meticulously devised by the school as well as by the then Gender Ministry. However, this problem continues to plague the Republic.

The other societal issue confronting Maldives was related to the increasing problem of divorce. It is significant to note that Maldives has the highest rate of divorce in the world. The extent of divorce according to different age groups is mentioned in Table 5.3.

Table 5.3 : Number of Persons Married and Divorced in Male by Age Group of Bride and Groom-2005 (in %)

Age Group	*Married*	*Divorced*
15-19	7.4	1.8
20-24	40.7	18.7
25-29	27.2	24.8
30.34	11.3	20.4
35-39	6.0	13.4
40-44	3.4	8.0
45-49	1.8	6.1
50 and Over	2.2	6.8

Source: Statistical Yearbook of Maldives, 2006, p. 50.

From the above table it appears that the maximum number of marriages took place in the age group 20-24 and large number of divorces was reported in the age group of 25-29. Further, in the age group of 25-29 the share of persons marrying and divorcing appeared to be nearly equal.

Even though divorce is not considered a stigma for a woman in Maldivian society, its existence affects the children emotionally. During discussions with children in some of the schools in Male, they mentioned poignantly that they were either living with their stepfather or stepmother. Few mentioned that they stayed with their grandparents. While children were not very vocal about how separation of their parents affected them, the manner in which they mentioned their immediate family and members constituting it, showed the pathos and emotional trauma that they were undergoing. When asked about their educational and occupational aspirations they appeared to be least interested about what they would like to do after they complete their school education.

Intake of drugs by children, especially adolescents, and adults was another social problem affecting the Republic. Children prone to taking drugs adversely affected the atmosphere of the family and the school. All the stakeholders reported that children prone to drugs indulged in criminal activities. Even though steps for addressing drug trafficking was taking by the government, schools and a few NGOs, this problem continues to exist, and was reported as a major issue of social tensions grappling the Republic.

Therefore, quality parameters related to education and social issues impacted the entire schooling ethos of Maldives.

Environment Degradation and the Rising Sea Level

Among all the nations of the world the Republic of Maldives faces a grave threat of its physical extinction. Global warming resulting in rising sea level has made the prospects of existence of this fragile nation, in the years to come, a watery graveyard.

Steps for addressing this natural calamity have been shared by the government at all forums at various national and international levels. The schools and community were also making attempts to address it. However, in all inhabited Islands felling of trees, growing construction of private and public offices and flats along with garbage disposal were some of the human activities that negatively impacted the natural habitat of this Island nation.

Thus the above-mentioned schooling factors along with environment issues have made quality a major challenge that needs to be addressed by the Republic. It is significant to note that most of the South Asian countries also face problems related to quality issues in education. However, the factors responsible for creating a paradox between quantity and quality in education vary from country to country. In the context of gender the major challenges that South Asian communities including Maldives face are related to grinding poverty of the household, violence against girls and women in the family, work place and the community. However, the natures of emotional and physical violence are once again at variance within and outside countries of South Asia and the worldover. In the context of education the mechanism for promoting gender harmony among sexes has been initiated in all countries both in the content and process of education. However, efforts in this regard are minuscule. Two recent studies in this regard Kirk (2008) and Page and Jha (2009) have highlighted that in countries of South Asia and some Commonwealth countries such as India, Malaysia, Nigeria, Pakistan, Samoa, Seychelles, Trinidad and Tobago have elements of bias and stereotyping in their schooling processes. This was mainly visible in teachers' and management's attitude and the materials prescribed to the children. Even though efforts were made by all the above-mentioned countries it was yet to get reflected in the textual materials and classroom practices to make education at all levels an empowering experience for both genders. Suggestive methods for rectifying biases and stereotypes in education, including violence against girls and women, have been suggested in both the studies for re-visiting their education policy, especially in the context of gender.

In the context of peace this study in Maldives highlighted that the focus was more on instilling peace as a value in children rather than stressing on peace as a skill for addressing the emerging social tensions and conflicts within and outside the school. Peace keeping strategies were stressed upon and minimal focus was on building in children skills of conflict resolution such as negotiation, consensus building and the art of learning to live together.

In fact peace as a strategy for addressing different forms of conflicts engulfing South Asia and SAARC countries in particular such as ethnic violence, drug peddling, trafficking of girls and women, feminisation of poverty, border disputes, teenage pregnancy and environment degradation and many more concerns are yet to be sensitively woven in the schooling processes that includes textual and supplementary materials, pedagogical processes and all curriculum plus activities such as debates, quiz, dance, drama, sports and physical education etc.

While efforts are being made in the context of Maldives and other South Asian countries including India, as stated earlier, a lot more conscious and committed initiatives need to be done both by the government and the civil society.

Specific Recommendations

The recommendations are based on the discussions held with the stakeholders in connection with content of textbooks and the overall schooling processes.

In the context of content, the specific suggestions were inclusion of themes on—Women Role Models, Continuity and Change in the Status of Women, Gender disaggregated data on Education, Demography, Social and Economic Indicators, Life and Conditions of the People of the Islands, History, Culture and Tradition of the Maldivian Society, Role of Regional and International Alliances in Connection with Learning to Live Together, Conservation and Preservation of Environment and Biographies of Asian leaders.

Regarding schooling processes some of the suggestions related to appointment of Counsellors in schools wherever they are needed, dissemination of career related information at the secondary stages, integration of life skills with education, strengthening resources of the library and linking it with internet, improving facilities in science labs, inclusion of swimming as an important sport, in service training programmes for social science, environmental studies and language teachers and for those handling children with special needs.

Strengthening the coordination between Educational Development Centre (EDC), Educational Supervision and Quality Improvement Section (ESQIS) and the Faculty of Education is essential for overall quality improvement in the teaching and learning processes.

REFERENCES

Cambridge Education: Strengthening the Framework of Education towards Vision 2020, Draft Final Report, Cambridge Education, 2005.

Kirk, Jackie, 2008. *Women Teaching in South Asia*, Sage Publication, New Delhi.

Page, Elspeth and Jha, Jyotsna, 2009. *Exploring the Bias, Gender and Stereotyping in Secondary Schools*, Commonwealth Secretariat, Marlborough House, London.

Seventh National Development Plan: 2006-2010 Maldives—Leaping Ahead: Vol. 1: Policies and Strategies, Ministry of Planning and National Development, Maldives, 2005.

Srivastava, Gouri, 2008. Gender and Peace: Education Policy, Curriculum English, Environment Studies and Social Studies Textbooks of the Republic of Maldives, project submitted to ASF (Unpublished).

Statistical Yearbook of Maldives, 2006. Ministry of Planning and National Development, Male.

APPENDIX I

Reflection of Women in Travel Accounts*

Laval, De Pyrard, Francois (1570-1621)

At nine years old they bring them up in the studies and exercises of the countrey. These studies are to learne to write and reade, and to understand their Alcoran, and know what they are bound to doe.their letters are divers sorts, the Arabicke with some letters and points which they have added to expresse their language: another where of character is peculiar to the language of the Maldives, and moreover, a third which is the vulgar of Ceylan, and of the greatest part of the Indies. They write their lessons on a little Table of wood, which are white, and when they can say their lessons by heart, they blot it out, and white it againe. If the writing bee to abide and remaine perpetually, they write upon Parhment which is made of the leafe of the tree called Macore Queau, which is a fathome and an halfe in length, and a foot broad. To teach their children to write, they have boards made of wood purposely, very smooth and plaine, whereon they spread very fine and thinne sand, after with a Bodkin they make the Letters, and make them imitate them, blotting out the Rule which they have written, and never use herein any paper. *(pp. 538-539)*

Idrisi, Sharif Al

All these Islands have a king, who unites them, protects and defends them, and makes truce according to his ability. His

* Vilgon Lars. 1991-94. *Maldive Odd History: The Maldive Archipelago and its People* Vols. 1-4. Stockholm.

wife acts as arbitrator among the people and does not veil herself from them. When she issues any order, her husband, the chief, although is present, does not interfere with any of her ordinances. It has always been a custom with them that women arbitrate, a custom from which they do not depart. This queen is called Dharma. She wears garments of woven gold, and her headwear is a crown of gold studded with various kinds of rubies and precious stones.

She wears gold sandals. In these Islands nobody wears sandals except this queen alone, and if anyone is found wearing sandals, his feet are amputated.

On ceremonial occasions and the feast days of her sect, this queen rides with her slave-girls behind her, in full procession of elephants, banners, and trumpets, while the king and all other Ministers follow her at a distance. This queen has riches, which she collects by means of certain known taxes, and she then gives in charity the wealth thus acquired to the needy inhabitants of her country on that day of her present and watching. Her subjects hang various kinds of silk garments along her routes and in the places she passes, and she wears magnificent attire. *(pp. 14-15)*

W. Young, I.A.

Though it would be thought improper to enter the private, or women's department, females are not kept from the view of strangers, or in a state of exclusions, as in most Mohammedan societies. They enjoy every reasonable liberty, of which, as well as of the kindness of their dispositions, we had pleasing evidence in a visit which we received from some ladies of rank during our sickness. They do not however eat along with men, but after them. Marriage is not very early engaged in, but a plurality of wives is allowed, few however, are able to support more than one wife, which decidedly contributes to the happiness of both parties. So far as we could observe, there prevailed very generally, a mutual affection between husband and wife. Intrigues however are not uncommon, and the men show no small ingénue in carrying them on, when the illicit correspondence is with a married woman. For a widow to live with a favourite without marriage is not accounted criminal and scarcely disgraceful.

Children of both sexes are required to read the Koran through, under the tuition of priests of the inferior order, and their lesson is begun very early, at three years of age. To be able to read, is all that appears to be thought. *(p. 141)*

Batuta, Ibn

Abn Alah Muhammad Ibn Batuta—he stayed at the Maldives from February/March of 1343 to the 26 of August 1344. He returned to Maldives for about a month in December 1346. This his own Arabic manuscript description of his life at the Maldives, translated into French by B. Defremery and C. Sangunetti. (Paris 1853-1855) Arabic.

The women of these Islands do not cover the head, the sovereign herself does not so. They comb their hair and tie it upon one right side of the head. *(p. 31)*

Sulaiman, Merchant

In these Islands, where a woman rules, cocoanut is cultivated. These islands are separated from one another by distance of two, three or four parasangs (3300-6600 metres). They are all inhabited, and they grow the coconut-trees in all of them. The wealth of the people is constituted by cowries, their Queen amasses large quantities of these cowries in the royal depots. They say that there is not in existence a people more industrious than these Islanders, so much so that they weave tunics of a single piece with two sleeves, two facings of the collar and the opening of the chest. They build shops, houses and execute all sorts of work with a consummate art. *(p. 5)*

Moresby, Robert

Robert Moresby was the commander of the surveying fleet sent out by the Honorable East India Company, in 1834-1836, to make the first accurate charts over the Maldives Islands. This is his own handwritten report about what he saw, heard and met in the Islands. It has never been published.

(English)

On this head our information is too limited to form a correct judgment, but I believe it is about the least that can be given when children are taught learn and write, they say that more women than men have attained that knowledge. *(p. 47)*

Robin, George

The population of Male may, I should think, be estimated at from 1,500 to 2000. The number of women exceeds that of the men. The greatest age that they live to is about 90 years—

"With regard to the state of education of the natives at the capital, of course our intercourse has been too limited, and too partial to form an opinion, I learn however that the women are more generally taught to read and write than the men, and that among the latter the knowledge of Arabic is by no means general even in the higher classes. Among the numerous monuments of mortality with which the Island abounds, I have seen but one with an Arabic inscription. *(pp. 55-57)*

Moresby, Robert

Children of both sexes are taught to read and write, and they are all expected to commit to memory the prayers and certain portions of the Koran. The teachers are either laymen or priests, and education, such as it is, is given gratis. *(p. 163)*

Women Rulers of Maldives

The present section gives a brief account of some of the women rulers of Maldives. A detailed account of the queens is mentioned. During their tenure the Island Nation was ably governed. This is mentioned in some travel accounts and in the writings of people who have written about this Island Nation.

Sultana Rehendi Khadijah
(748 AH/1347 AD to 778 AH/1377 AD)

Sultana Rehendi Khadijah was the eldest daughter of Sultan Jalaluddin Umar Veer. He was the son of Sultan Salahuddin who in turn was a son of a noble family from Bengal. Princess Rehendin Khadijah was married to Al-Qaleeb Mohamed Jamaluddin, her half brother. Ahmad Shihabuddin was ruling the kingdom of Maldives. His manners, behaviour and attitude were very unlike a leader, and therefore, he was very unpopular among his subjects. Historians mention that he was finally exiled to a far off Island named Hadummati and he died there. In 748 AH after the death of Ahmad Shihabuddin, Rehendi Khadijah occupied the ruling seat and acquired the title of Sultana Rehendi Khadijah Kanbaidhi Kilege Sri Lok Abarana.

During her reign she married thrice. A detailed mention about her administrative policy is available in travel accounts of the famous traveller Ibn Batuta who visited Maldives during the second year of her reign. He mentions that this Island kingdom was in urgent need of a qazi who could look into cases and give judgments according to Islamic Sharia. He adds that when he visited Maldives, Sultana Rehendi Khadijah appointed him as the Qazi of the Island.

A glimpse of the historical past of Maldives can be acquired from his travel notes. Ibn Batuta mentions that people of Maldives during his stay did not use paper for purposes of writing. Written work was mainly done on the coconut leaf, with the help of a sharp knife or any other sharp object. He also mentions that people who wanted to meet the Sultan were required to bring two bundles of expensive cloth and respectfully bow before her and her husband who was also the Prime Minister. Her palace was known as *Daar*. In his travel notes Ibn Batuta mentions about the military preparedness of the Sultana. He states that she had more than 1000 soldiers who were always kept in a state of constant fitness. These soldiers used to pay their respects to Sultana daily. The Sultana's army was paid in kind, i.e. rice every month and this was procured from the government godown. All the thousand soldiers used to have separate attendance for the salary. News about the military strength was given to the Sultana regularly through the Prime Minster. Based on the attendance, soldiers were given rice according to their designation. Regular salutations were given to her by all Ministers including the Qazi and the Prime Minister. In the initial years of her reign she handled all the business of the government independently; gradually her husband took over the charge. However, in all important matters of the state she took independent decisions. All orders of the state were passed by her. The Sultana's name was taken in Friday Prayers. The content of the prayer was as follows:

May God help his Maid to whom he has given the power to rule on behalf of the people of the whole Muslim community i.e. Sultan Rehendi Khadijah.

This prayer was recited loudly so that everyone in the Island could listen. When Sultana Rehendi Khadijah completed 16 years of her reign, i.e. 748 AH/1347AD to 764 AH/1363 AD, her husband conspired with a few people to get hold over the crown and removed his wife, Sultana Rehendi Khadijah. However, he was not successful in his endeavour. Some historians have a different version to state. According to them Rehendi Khadijah killed her husband and occupied the throne of Maldives.

The Second Phase of her Reign

The second phase of the reign of Sultana begins from 1365 AD. During her second tenure she ruled for a period of 10 years. In this phase she married Ahdullah-ibn Mohammead al-Maqrami, her Prime Minister. During this period Ibn Batuta once again visited Maldives. This time he stayed in an Island called Kanodes. The Island chief was Aziz al Maqdashawi, who was very lenient and merciful. Ibn Batuta writes in his tour diary that the leader of Kanodes Island gave a big party in his honour and after that he also made the arrangements of his travel to the capital of Maldives, i.e. Male. On his sojourn to Male he also visited different Islands, especially the one where the Sultana would visit with her family members and companions regularly. This particular Island was of scenic beauty. It did not have many trees but the surroundings of the Island comprised white sand which twinkled in the hot sun. This particular Island was known as Halwale. During the royal retreat in this Island a small kind of sport was held called *Tatjar*. For observing this sport many guests would visit the Island including top ranking officers and Ministers. The entire guests visiting the Island would give the Sultana gifts. Ibn Batuta met the sister of Rehendi Khadijah in this particular Island and later married her.

Sultana Rehendi Khadijah's stepson Khateeb Mohammed Ankafan met Ibn Batuta on the Island of Halwale. Once again the traveller was well treated by the people of Maldives. He was given a party in the Island where Mohammed Ankafan resided. Some of the people of the Island were sent to Male for informing the people and those in administration of his arrival. In Male, one of the Ministers was very interested about his whereabouts, he was none other than Abdullah Kalige. He directed his officials to make good arrangements for his stay. Thus, the traveller was very well treated.

Ibn Batuta's second visit was guided by personal considerations. He wanted to take his two-year-old son born from a Maldivian woman. He writes:

Sultana Rehendi Khadija's Prime Minister, Abdullah Kalige gave me a very warm welcome. Further, he gifted me with some expensive clothes, roses and pan which were an indication of friendship and close bonding during this period. He mentions that he reciprocated the warm gesture shown by giving the two bundles of silk cloth to the Prime Minister.

Thus, from the travel accounts of Ibn Batuta it appears that the reigns of Rehendi Khadijah were periods marked by cultural development and growth. Further, the business of the government was run very smoothly. All the posts of the administration were held by people of noble birth.

Sultana Rehendi Khadijah's second phase lasted 10 years from 1363 to 1374 AD. Her second phase was once again marked by unfortunate developments on the family front. Her second husband forcefully tried to seize the throne. Sultana Rehendi Khadijah was aware of her husband's intentions. She was very clear about herself and her position. She was determined to continue as a ruler. With great skilfulness and planning she eliminated her husband, and thus befittingly paid him for his treachery and his unfaithfulness to her.

Thus, after eliminating her husband she once again retained the throne of the kingdom in her name. Her third term was from 1374 AD to 1377 AD. During this period she got married for the third time. This time her husband was Ali Handigeri. From all her three marriages she did not have any issue. The reign of Sultana Rehendi Khadijah lasted for a total period of 29 years.

Besides, Rehendi Khadijah, Maldives had the fortune of having two other women rulers. A brief account is stated below:

Sultana Raadafathi Kilege Sri Suwem Abarana

She was the second daughter of Umar Veer Jalauddin and also the stepsister of Rehendi Khadijah. She was married to K. Mohammed Tarkufan. She ruled for a very short period, i.e. four months—781 AH to 782 AH. As in the case of her stepsister her husband also seized the throne.

Sultana Dhain Kanbaidhi Kilege Sri Suwarna

She was the daughter of Sultan Mohammed al Makerti. She ruled for four years from 1384 AD to 1388 AD and then her own husband who was the Prime Minister Abdullah took over as the ruler of Maldives.

Source: The text is written by Habeeba Hussain Habeeba and translated by Noor Alam, Project Fellow, Department of Women's Studies, NCERT, New Delhi.

APPENDIX III

Tools for Textbook Evaluation and Classroom Processes

A. Tools for Textbook Evaluation

Identification Data

1. Title of the textbook
2. Class
3. Subject
4. Language
5. Authors (s)
6. Editors (s)
7. Month and Year of Publication
8. Total no. of pages
9. *(a) Cover/Back pages: Visuals*

Sl. No. Visuals Portraying	Women/ Girls	Men/ Boys	Both	None
1. **Students**				
2. **Educationalist**				
3. **Professionals**				
4. **Producers**				
5 **Role models**				
6. **Artist/Theatre Persons**				
7. **Social reformers**				
8. **Leaders representing historical and contemporary movements**				
9. **Animal/Birds species depicted as**				
10. **Natural habitat**				
11. **Any other**				

9. *(b) Cover/Back pages: Content*

Content	Women/Girls	Men/Boys	Both	None
Sayings and Quotations related to				
Messages				
Any other				

10. *Symbolic Representation of Colours*

11. *Any other Features Related to Identities: Such as*
National

Religious

Linguistic

Neutral

12. *Whether Contextualisation has been taken care of*

13. *Organisation of the themes*

B. Content Analysis Chapter-wise
Chapter/Lesson No:
Theme:
Total no. of pages:

Sl. No.	*Criteria*	*Men/ Boys*	*Women/ Girls*	*Both*	*No. of Times*
1.	**Adjectives used for both sexes**				
2.	**Pronoun/common words used/names**				
3.	**Occupations** • **Primary** • **Tertiary** • **Service sector**				
4.	**Roles** • **Administrators** • **Decision-makers** • **Leaders** • **Producers** • **Social reformers** • **Educationalists** • **Any other**				
5.	**Values associated with both sexes**				
6.	**Derogatory remarks used**				
7.	**Men and women depicted in relational terms (father of, mother of, sister of, wife of, daughter of.....)**				
8.	**Mention of exiting customary practices** • ***Purdah*** • **Child marriage** • **Female foetecide** • **Trafficking of women** • **Dowry** • **Any other**				
9.	**Any other localised practices mentioned**				
10.	**Mention of violence:** • **Physical** • **Emotional**				

C. Does the chapter mention conflicting situations in:

- The family
- School
- Classroom
- Community
- Work place
- National level
- International level
- Any other

D. Who takes initiatives in resolving conflicts

— Men in different capacities
— Women in different capacities
— Both
— State
— Non-Governmental Agencies
— Any other

E. What methods are adopted for conflict resolution

— Power assertions
— Consensus
— Delay/Postponement
— Suggest constructive solutions
— Laws
— Any other

F. Is there a mention of Human Rights then which Right are mentioned?

G. Rights pertaining to Men/Boys

H. Rights pertaining to Women/Girls

I. Duties pertaining to Men/Boys

J. Duties pertaining to Women/Girls

K. Visuals in the Lesson

Criteria	*Male*	*Female*	*Both*	*None*
Role models				
Professionals				
Fine arts				
Any other				

L. Evaluation Exercises based on Gender and Peace

Criteria's	*Male*	*Female*	*Both*	*None*
Knowledge				
Understanding of Gender and Peace				
Skills related to Communication Negotiation Critical thinking				
Ethics and Values				

M. Perception of Lesson/Chapter from the viewpoint of

- Gender Bias
- Gender Stereotyping
- Gender Inclusive
- Gender Neutral
- Conflict Management/Peaceful co-existence

N. Points of discussion with students on

- Visuals
- Contents
- Illustrations
- Exercises

Tools for Assessing Physical Facilities and Schooling Processes

1. Name of the School :
2. Location :
3. Level : Lower/Secondary/Senior Secondary/Any other
4. Type : Co-education/Single Sex
5. Managed by : Government/Private/Community Support

Existing Physical Facilities in Schools [Please put or tick (√) mark]

Facilities	*Stages*	*Boys*	*Girls*	*Both*
Boundary Wall				
Classrooms				
Electricity				
Ventilation				
Furniture				
Desks				
Chairs				
Blackboard				
Notice Board				
Drinking Water				
Toilets				
Library Room				
Reference Books				
Prayer Room				
Playground				
Health Facilities • First-Aid Box • Medical Room				
Canteen				
Sports Equipments				
Any Other				

Subjects Offered at Different Grades (Primary, Secondary, Senior Secondary)

Sl. No.	*Subjects*	*Boys*	*Girls*	*Both*

Existing Motivational Schemes (Primary, Secondary, Senior Secondary)

Sl. No.	Motivational Schemes	Boys	Girls	Both	Availabilities			
					Y	M	W	D

Enrolments Stage-wise Grades

Sl. No.	Year	Boys	Girls	Total

Classroom Processes (Primary)

Sl. No.	*Classroom Management*	*Boys*	*Girls*	*Both*
1.	Sitting Arrangements • Random • Mixed • Separate			
2.	Teaching Learning Materials available • Textbooks • Supplementary/Resource materials • Stationery items • Any other			
3.	Bulletin Boards • User friendly • Not user friendly			
4.	Roles Assigned • Boys • Girls • Both			
5.	Monitors • Boys • Girls • Both			
6	Assignment of Responsibility			
7.	Cleaning Classrooms, Blackboard, Bulletin Board, any other			
8.	Getting water, chalk, duster, copies, books, registers, any other			
9.	Leaders of different groups Academic groups such as—Debates and quiz, reading, writing, essay, any other			
10.	Cultural Group such as—Music, dance, any other			
11.	Any other activities			
12.	Participation in classrooms			
13.	Questioning			
14.	Answering • Frequently • Sometimes • Not responding			
15.	Providing Additional Information • Frequently • Sometimes • Not responding			
16.	Any other			

Hidden Curriculum in Classrooms (for Teacher)

Sl. No.	*Criteria Hidden Current*	*Boys*	*Girls*	*Both*
1.	Eye Contact			
2.	Hand Gestures			
3.	Facial Expressions			
4.	Language used for communication • Pleasant • Derogatory • Harsh • Satisfactory • No comments			
5.	Posture • Sitting • Standing • Walking			
6.	Any other			

Any images of gender bias and conflict which gets reflected in teacher talk and student responses

Visible Human Values in Teaching and Learning Process

Sl. No.	*Values*	*Related to Content*	*Specially imparted by mentioning role models and their contribution*	*Through Activities*	*Personal Examples*	*Any other*
1.	Sharing and carrying					
2.	Equality between sexes					
3.	Valuing each other's contributions (men/women)					
4.	Dignity of labour					
5.	Tolerance					
6.	Bravery					
7.	Honesty					
8.	Patriotism					
9.	Non-violence • Speech • Action					
10.	Any other					

Time Schedule of a School

1.	Assembly
2.	Time assigned for different subjects __________ __________ __________ __________
3.	Activities • Music • Dance • Debates • Sports • Indoor • Outdoor • Any other __________ __________ __________
4.	Hobbies __________ __________ __________ __________
5.	Remedial Teaching
6.	Lunch
7.	Any other schedule of the school

Details of curriculum plus activities designed for boys and girls

Sl. No.	*Criteria*	*Boys*	*Girls*	*Both*
1.	Sewing			
2.	Knitting			
3.	Handicraft			
4.	Clay Modelling			
5.	Carpentry			
6.	Reading			
7.	Writing			
8.	Dancing			
9.	Debates			
10.	Vocal Music			
11.	Instrumental Music			
12.	Computers			
13.	Any other			

Addressing behavioural issues concerning both gender

Sl. No.	*Criteria*	*Boys*	*Girls*	*Both*
1.	Counselling			
2.	Peer group interactions			
3.	Disciplinary measures			
4.	Discussing with parents			
5.	Punishments			
6.	Any other			
7.	None of the above			

Overall observation of the school

Classroom/outside classroom activities are:

I. Gender Biased

II. Gender Stereotyped

III. Gender Inclusive

Strategies for addressing conflicts and social tensions

Tools for lesson observation form

Teacher Name: School:

Grade: Number of students:

Subject: Lesson:

Please put a tick (√) mark

	Excellent	*Good*	*Satis-factory*	*Needs improve-ment*	*Not obser-ved*
Lesson Plan					
Clear and appropriate learning objectives					
Logical sequence of steps					
Classroom organisation					
Activities linked to objectives					
Use of appropriate teaching materials					
Self-evaluation					
Lesson Presentation					
Teacher's manner is confident and relaxed					
Appropriate use of time					
Knowledge of subject content					
Established open-ended problem solving					
Coordinated multiple student responses					
Students communicated with their peers and the teacher					
Students worked collaboratively					
Students' errors were corrected					
Students used manipulatives					
Connected local examples to the lesson					
Made connections to other topics					
Made connections to other content areas					

Classroom Management					
Teacher authority established and accepted					
Awareness of classroom events					
Monitoring pupil activity					
Interacts with individual students as well as small groups					
Teacher's movement in class					
Students on task					
Manages disruptive behaviour appropriately					
Relationship with Students					
Rapport, warmth and enthusiasm					
Variety in interactive pattern					
Welcomes students' questions					
Reinforcement and feedback					

Additional Comments:

Strengths

Weaknesses

Recommendations

Observer's Name:
Signature:
Date:

Source: Ministry of Education, Educational Supervision and Quality Improvement Section.

Questionnaire for the Principal [Please put a tick (√) mark]

1. Name of the school:

___

___

2. Levels: Primary, Secondary

___

___

3. Name: ___
4. Age less than 30 ( ), 31-35 ( ), 36-40 ( ), 41-45 ( )
   46-50 ( ), 51-55 ( ), 56-60 ( ), Above 61 ( )

5. Marital Status: Single ( ), Married ( )
   Separated ( ), Divorced ( )
   Widowed ( )

6. Nationality ___

7. Qualification
   Educational
   Professional

___

8. Vision about Gender Equality

___

9. Vision in the Context of Peace

___

10. Vision regarding Conflict Management and Social Tensions

___

Questionnaire for the Teachers [Please put a tick (√) mark]

1. Name of the School
2. Levels — Primary, Middle, Lower Secondary, Upper Secondary
3. Teacher's Name
4. Age — Less than 30 ( ), 31-35 ( ), 36-40 ( ), 41-45 ( ) 46-50 ( ), 51-55 ( ), 56-60 ( ), Above 61 ( )

5. Marital Status — Single ( ), Married ( ), Separated ( ), Divorced ( ), Widowed ( )

6. Nationality
7. Qualification
   Education
   Professional

8. Subject taught:
9. Do you think the textbooks you use for teaching are
   Gender Biased:
   Stereotyped:
   Gender Neutral:
   Address issue of Peace:
   No comments:

10. In your view who participates more in classroom activities
    Boys ( ) Girls ( ) Both ( )

    Why this pattern?

11. Who provides additional information related to lessons taught?
    Boys ( ) Girls ( ) Both ( )

12. Whom do you appoint as class monitors?
    Boys ( ) Girls ( ) Both ( )

13. Whom do you assign the following task?

(a)	Cleaning the classroom	Boys	Girls	Both
(b)	Cleaning the Blackboard	Boys	Girls	Both
(c)	Bringing water, duster, chalk, charts etc.	Boys	Girls	Both

14. What is your educational aspirations for—
Boys Girls Both
Ans. ....
15. What kind of professions you want children to take up?
Boys Girls Both
Ans. ....
16. Kind of values do you want children to imbibe?

Sl. No.	*Values*	*Boys*	*Girls*	*Both*
1	Caring and sharing			
2	Equality between sexes			
3	Obedience			
4	Respectfulness			
5	Silence			
6	Tolerance			
7	Dignity of labour			
8	Valuing women's contribution			
9	Patriotion			
10	Non-violence in Speech Action			
11	Honesty			
12	Truthfulness			
13	Respecting other's religion			
14	Respecting National Symbols			
15	Duties towards Nation			
16	Cleanliness			
17	Punctuality			
18	Human Rights			
19	Learning to live together			

17. In your opinion what type of roles do you expect boys and girls to take up?

Sl. No.	Roles	Boys	Girls	Both	Reasons
1	Leadership				
2	Decision-maker Home School Workplace				
3	Conventional				
4	Unconventional				
5	Any other				

18. In your opinion what type of co-curricular activities do children of your school participate in?

Sl. No.	Roles	Boys	Girls	Both	Reasons
1	Dance				
2	Drama				
3	Debates				
4	Music Vocal Instrumental				
5	Recitation				
6	Quiz				
7	Any other				

19. In your opinion do children of your school participate in the following sports/physical activities?

Sl. No.	Sports/Physical Activities	Boys	Girls	Both	Reasons
1	Indoor • Carrom board • Ludo • Any other				
2	Outdoor Any other				

20. How do you tackle problems related to violence in your class, both physical and verbal?
21. In your opinion how can gender harmony be promoted in your classroom activities and outside classroom activities?

Classroom

Outside Classroom

MINISTRY OF EDUCATION
MALÉ, REPUBLIC OF MALDIVES

ACADEMIC CALENDAR 2007

Term	Duration	No. of Days
Term 1	14 Jan. to 12 Apr.	63*
Term 2	23 Apr. to 25 Jul.	68
Term 3	5 Aug. to 15 Nov.	72
	Total	203

MONTH	S	M	T	W	T	F	S	CALENDAR DATES	PUBLIC HOLIDAYS
JANUARY		1	2	3	4	5	6	10 January, Teachers' Reporting Day	1-2 January, New Year Day/Occasion of Eid Al'haa
	7	8	9	10	11	12	13	A' Level (Edexcel) Examinations (10 - 29 Jan)	
	[illegible]	15	16	17	18	19	20	14 Jan, Academic Year 2007 Begins	20 January, Islamic New Year (1428)
	21	22	23	24	25	26	27		
	28	29	30	31	1	2	3		
FEBRUARY	4	5	6	7	8	9	10		
	11	12	13	14	15	16	17		
	18	19	20	21	22	23	24		
	25	26	27	28	1	2	3		
MARCH	4	5	6	7	8	9	10		
	11	12	13	14	15	16	17		
	18	19	20	21	22	23	24		20 March, National Day
	25	26	27	28	29	30	31	25 Mar - 5 Apr, First Term Test (Secondary)	31 March, Prophet Mohamed's Birthday
APRIL	1	2	3	4	5	6	7	1 - 5 Apr, First Term Test (Primary)	
	8	9	10	11	12	13	14	12 Apr, End of Term 1	
	15	16	17	18	19	20	21	15 - 19 Apr, First Term Holidays	20 April, Day to Mark Maldives Embracement to Islam
	22	23	24	25	26	27	28	23 Apr, Term 2 Begins	22 April, as 20 April falls on Friday
	29	30	1	2	3	4	5		
MAY	6	7	8	9	10	11	12		
	13	14	15	16	17	18	19	A' Level (Edexcel) & HSC Examinations	
	20	21	22	23	24	25	26	(14 May - 29 Jun)	
	27	28	29	30	31	1	2		
JUNE	3	4	5	6	7	8	9		
	10	11	12	13	14	15	16		
	17	18	19	20	21	22	23		
	24	25	26	27	28	29	30	24 June, Higher Secondary Academic Year Begins	
JULY	1	2	3	4	5	6	7		
	8	9	10	11	12	13	14	8 - 19 July, Second Term Test (Secondary)	
	15	16	17	18	19	20	21	15 - 19 July, Second Term Test (Primary)	
	22	23	24	25	26	27	28	25 July, End of Term 2	26 July, Independence Day
	29	30	31	1	2	3	4	29 July - 2 Aug, Second Term Holidays	27 July, Occasion of Independence Day
AUGUST	5	6	7	8	9	10	11	5 Aug, Term 3 Begins	
	12	13	14	15	16	17	18		
	19	20	21	22	23	24	25		
	26	27	28	29	30	31	1		
SEPTEMBER	2	3	4	5	6	7	8		
	9	10	11	12	13	14	15		13 September, First of Ramazan
	16	17	18	19	20	21	22		
	23	24	25	26	27	28	29		
OCTOBER	30	1	2	3	4	5	6		
	7	8	9	10	11	12	13		12 Oct, Eid Al-Fithri
	14	15	16	17	18	19	20	O'Level, IGCSE & SSC Examinations (15Oct-15Nov)	13 - 14 Oct, Occasion of Eid Al-Fithri
	21	22	23	24	25	26	27	21 Oct - 8 Nov, Third Term Test (Secondary)	
	28	29	30	31	1	2	3		3 November, Victory Day
NOVEMBER	4	5	6	7	8	9	10	4 - 8 Nov, Third Term Test (Primary)	
	11	12	13	14	15	16	17	15 Nov, End of Academic Year 2007	11 November, Republic Day
	18	19	20	21	22	23	24		
	25	26	27	28	29	30	1		
DECEMBER	2	3	4	5	6	7	8		
	9	10	11	12	13	14	15		
	16	17	18	19	20	21	22		19 Dec, Hajj Day. 20 Dec, Eid Al'haa
	23	24	25	26	27	28	29		21- 23 December, Occasion of Eid Al'haa
JANUARY (2008)	30	31	1	2	3	4	5		1 January, New Year Day (2008)
	6	7	8	9	10	11	12	8 January, Teachers' Reporting Day	
	[illegible]	14	15	16	17	18	19	13 Jan, Academic Year 2008 Begins	

School Days Public Holidays Weekends Term Holidays School Exam Days

* One day reduced from the total number of days of First Term as Opening of Citizens' Majlis falls in First Term.

Bibliography

Bell, H.C.P. 1940. *The Maldive Islands: Monograph on the History, Archaeology and Epigraphy*. Ceylon Government Press, Colombo.

Bourdieu, Pierre and Passeron, J.C. 1990. *Reproduction in Education, Society and Culture*. Sage Publication: New Delhi.

Cambridge Education: Strengthening the Framework of Education Towards Vision 2020, Draft Final Report, 2005, Male, Maldives.

CEDAW: Achievements and Challenges in the Maldives: Ministry of Women's Affairs and Social Security, August 2002, Male, Maldives.

Dias, Edward. 1949. The Maldives Islands. Ministry of External Affairs: Maldive Islands, Maldives.

Giroux, A. Henry. 1981. Ideology Culture and the Process of Schooling. The Falmer Press: London.

Hayward, Ruth Finney. 2000. Breaking the Earthenware Jar: Lessons from South Asia to End Violence against Women. UNICEF.

Hockly, T.W. 1940. *The Two Thousand Isles: A Short Account of the People, History and Customs of the Maldive Archipelago*. Witherby: London.

Jha, D.N. 1981. *Ancient India: An Introductory Outline*. New Delhi: People's Publishing House.

King, M. Elizabeth and Hill, M. Anne (eds.). 1991. *Women's Education in Developing Countries: Barriers, Benefits and Policy*. World Bank.

Kirk, Jackie. 2008. *Women Teaching in South Asia*, Sage Publication: New Delhi.

Kumar, Krishna. 2001. *Prejudice and Pride: School Histories of the Freedom Struggle in India and Pakistan*. Viking: New Delhi.

Learning: The Treasure within, Report to UNESCO of the International Commission on Education for the 21st Century, UNESCO Publishing, 1996.

Maldives: 25 Years of Independence 1965-1990, Published by Media Transasia Ltd. Bangkok, 1990.

Maloney, Clarence. 1980. *People of the Maldive Islands*. Orient Longman: New Delhi.

Mohamed, Naseema. 2006. *Essays on Early Maldives*. Male: Maldives.

Muslehuddin, Mohammad. 1999. Sociology and Islam: A Comparative Study of Islam and its Social System. Islamic Book Trust: Kuala Lumpur, Malaysia.

Nahid, Shakir. 2001. *Maya Dhaitha: A Maldivian Folktale*. Educational Development Centre, Ministry of Education. Impress Print: Male, Maldives.

Neville, Adrian, Dhivehi Raajje. 1993-95. A Portrait of Maldives, Seven Holidays.

Page, Elspeth and Jha, Jyotsna. 2009. *Exploring the Bias, Gender and Stereotyping in Secondary Schools*. Commonwealth Secretariat: Marlborough House, London.

Phadnis, U., Luithui, E.D. 1985. *Maldives Winds of Change in an Atoll State*. South Asian Publishers: New Delhi.

Pyrard, The Voyage of Francois Pyrard of Laval to the East Indies, the Maldives, the Moluccas, and Brazil. Trans. Albert Gray, 2 Vols. London, Hakluyt Society, 1888. Original editions 1611, 1615, and 1619.

School Statistics 2005. Ministry of Education, Republic of Maldives.

Seventh National Development Plan 2006-2010: Maldives—Leaping Ahead, Vol. 1, Policies and Strategies, Maldives, Male, Ministry of Planning and National Development, Ghazee Building.

Srivastava, Gouri. 2000. *Women's Higher Education in the 19th Century*. Concept Publishing Company Pvt. Ltd.: New Delhi.

Statistical Year Book of Maldives, 2006. Ministry of Planning and National Development, Male, Maldives.

Status of the Girl-Child and Women, 2006, Republic of Maldives, Ministry of Gender and Family.

Tawil, Sobhi and Harley, Alexandra. 2004. *Education, Conflict and Social Cohesion*. International Bureau of Education, UNESCO, Geneva.

Vilgon, Lars. 1991-1998. Maldive Odd History: The Maldive Archipalago and its People, Vol. 4: Stockholm.

Unpublished Documents

The Framework of the National Curriculum: 1999, Draft of Unofficial Translation. Male.

The Draft Syllabus for English in the National Curriculum, October 2004, Educational Development Centre, Male, Maldives.

Primary School, Syllabus for Social Studies. Male.

Index

AN INTRODUCTION TO

FISHES